Love Apples Too

Cover: View to Jethou from the grounds of Les Côtils on the occasion of the conference 'International Computer Archive of Modern and Medieval English', held there in May 2003. Photo courtesy Dr. Ute Römer, University of Michigan

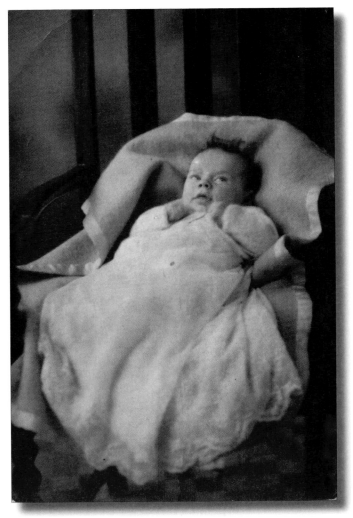

The author in 1942, aged three months

Love Apples Too

... A Life in Guernsey

Yvonne Ozanne

author of *Love Apple Island*, 2007

Foreword by Professor Edward Chaney

ELSP

Published in 2009 by
ELSP
16A New St John's Road
St Helier
Jersey   JE2 3LD

Origination by Seafower Books, Jersey

Printed in Britain by
Cromwell Press Group
Trowbridge, Wiltshire

ISBN 978-1-906641-15-3

For my best beloved

And to my mother Mary Bréhaut with love

CONTENTS

Foreword by Professor Edward Chaney   8

Introduction   11

Acknowledgements   12

1   Another Story   13

2   Dressing Up   16

3   Herm, a Paradise   19

4   A Lovesome Thing   23

5   Christmas Stars   26

6   Firelight   30

7   Family Roots   34

8   Ebenezer: Stone of Help   37

9   Guernsey born: G.B. Edwards and the Heaumes   41

10   Sweet Chariots   45

11   Diamond Days   48

12   Snow White   51

13   Forest Clan   54

14   The Wireless   57

15   A Kind of Living   60

16   To Be a Guern   63

17   Summer Days   66

18   Isabella   69

19   Budloe, Nipper and Titch   72

20   Sark   75

21   Cloud of Iona   79

22   Imagination Counts   82

23   An Opening Door   85

24   For the Love of Art   90

25	Our Vale Church	94
26	Finding Sanctus	97
27	Alderney	101
28	Alderney Visited	105
29	Houmet Paradis	110
30	Death of a Market	113
31	Babis's Apples	116
32	Get Fresh	120
33	Adèle Hugo	124
34	Vive la Différence	128
35	Of Clams and Camping	131
36	French Exchange	135
37	Venice with Nina and Kate	139
38	Guernsey Literature and Potato Peel Pie	145
39	Tide and Time	149
40	Mary Bréhaut	153
41	A Matter of Manners	157

FOREWORD

YVONNE OZANNE AND THE CULTURAL MEMORY OF GUERNSEY

by Edward Chaney

In these unpretentious but profound, 'charming' yet insightful essays, Yvonne Ozanne immortalizes a world that hovers on the cusp of being lost for ever. One emerges from reading them, however, with the feeling that for as long as it remains inhabited, Guernsey is unlikely to lose its collective or cultural memory, even if this memory might depend for its survival as much on its appreciative immigrants as on native Guerns. Hailing from Irish as well as Guernsey stock, Yvonne has the advantage of being both fully integrated in island life as well as gifted with that element of objectivity or 'otherness' that is the hallmark of the best journalists.

But the sum of the parts has become more than mere journalism. Yvonne's very evocative essays, first published individually in the *Guernsey Press* and now collected in book format, constitute an important means by which Guernsey's cultural memory may be sustained. Local traditions, once passed down the generations via customary acts and word of mouth, now tend to be enervated by various forms of global media. They thus depend increasingly on the written word for their sustenance and it is largely via this older medium (though recorded oral history and film have roles to play) that the past may remain part of, and enrich, the present. Meanwhile, the present's perception of the past evolves unpredictably, though I remain un-persuaded by academic theories that insist that the past is actually altered by the present. It is the duty of the historian to re-evoke, and then interpret, an objective past as truthfully as possible.

This book of essays, the second in what I hope will be a continuing series of Love Apples, is full of nostalgia, occasionally sentiment and – within healthily sceptical limits – love for the author's island home. I am honoured to be asked to succeed that great, Guernsey-born actor Roy Dotrice, who introduced Yvonne's first volume in 2007. I got to know Roy after his superb serialized reading on Radio 4 of *The Book of Ebenezer Le Page*, the creation of an even older friend, Gerald Edwards, who left me the typescript of his masterpiece, which I eventually got published in 1981.

8

Gerald, who wrote his great, one-off, testamentary novel in a similar spirit to that in which Lampedusa wrote about Sicily in *The Leopard*, expressed an even more conflicted love for his native island. Perhaps because he felt exiled, having been effectively disinherited by his father, as well as the love he felt a correspondingly greater scepticism, sometimes bordering on scorn, particularly for local officialdom. Despite (or because of?) having spent most of his adult life in England, he emotionally identified with Guernsey but at the same time treated his *Sarnia Cherie* as if she were a cross between his mother and a beautiful whore who had inadequately reciprocated his love for her. In his magnificent novel, which he in fact entitled *Sarnia Cherie*, his *alter ego*, Ebenezer, expressed his frustrated love for 'this whore of an island' in parallel with what he felt for Liza Queripel, whom at one point, during the German occupation, he indeed accuses of being a whore or 'jerry bag'. He is ultimately reconciled to Liza, however, and discovers they were vicariously united via their illegitimate grandchildren, her descendant being the Neville Falla to whom Ebenezer bequeaths his Book; his being Neville's lover, Adèle (the name of Victor Hugo's daughter to whom Yvonne devotes one of her most interesting essays). However anti-Romantic or resistant to sentiment readers may think they are, I defy anyone not to be moved to tears by Gerald's account of Ebenezer's last meeting with Liza. This is the prelude to his farewells to Neville, Guernsey and to life itself. Before he falls asleep for the last time he stays up late, completing the last of his three journals:

> I wish I could have my life again. I wish I could write my story again. I have judged people. I do not want to judge people. I want to bless. I want to bless every soul who have ever lived and laughed and suffered on this whore of an island, this island in the sun, this island in God's sea.

Yvonne shares something of Gerald's ambivalence where the island culture is concerned but in her two essays on *The Book of Ebenezer Le Page* she shows that she fully appreciates Guernsey's greatest cultural creation. The same may not be said about the Guernsey establishment. I am indeed informed that recently the States distributed multiple copies of the American Mary Ann Shaffer's *Guernsey Literarary and Potato Peel Society* as a free gift. They thus exceeded any equivalent effort they had made for more than a quarter of a century to promote the far more authentic *Book of Ebenezer Le Page*. Perhaps their reluctance is the result of too literal a reading of Ebenezer's complaints about modern Guernsey or the more overt critique with which Gerald concluded his novel in his appendix on 'Guernsey English'? It still seems extraordinary to me that the potential for G.B. Edwards to be for Guernsey what Hardy is to Dorset and James Joyce is to Dublin, has not been realised. Even after the great success of Joyce Cook's two theatrical versions, *Ebenezer* still fails to merit a mention on the Tourist Board's complimentary DVD. Would not a less numerous but more selective class of no doubt wealthier cultural tourist not improve the island? When in the 1980s I failed to persuade the Guernsey Tourist Board to help fund a film of *Ebenezer Le Page* it was subsidising Power Boar Racing on the assumption this would prove more popular. It reminds me of the campaign I have been fighting all summer to prevent Southampton's councillors from selling major works of art belonging to the City Art Gallery in order to build a Titanic Museum.

But despite occasional disgust with a foul-mouthed yob or the destruction of an historic building, Yvonne's broad-mindedness is more evenly distributed than Ebenezer's, being well-enough connected to the modern (and non-Guern) world to use E-bay and critique TV comedy not to speak of French or Venetian restaurants and art galleries. It is, however, always to Guernsey she returns for comparison and her deepest philosophical understanding. In his Guernsey English appendix, dated 31 July 1974, Gerald wrote that 'It is doubtful whether any Guernseyman alive anywhere on the island today feels and thinks like Ebenezer Le Page.' Clearly, he specified 'on the island' as he himself no longer was. Though taken off it as a child, Yvonne has since been unerringly 'on the island'.

Without being too Ebenezerish for contemporary taste, there is a related, deeply conservative quality to her loyalty to almost every aspect of her grandparents' Guernsey way of life and her corresponding impatience with most aspects of the modern world's incursions against the civilization she loves and strives to defend. As in Gerald's novel, these essays depict a specific island in all its vivid beauty and particularity. Individual friends and family members are described with great humanity. But the aspects of both island and people that the author chooses to write about and the care with which she does so makes all such particulars universal so that there is nothing here that should not be of interest to the discerning reader anywhere.

Southampton
1 September 2009

INTRODUCTION

Guernsey people and all Channel Islanders share a love of our beautiful and precious islands, survivors of the German Occupation of World War Two. The close communities and places we cherish will live on in shared memories of our deeply rooted, unique culture.

When I published *Love Apple Island* in 2007, I hoped that at least a small record of our lives might be preserved. You have agreed in your thousands, from all over the globe. *Love Apples Too* continues this hope.

It is our privilege to live here and belong to such a special place in the world. We look to the future with pride. *A La Prochaine!*

Yvonne Ozanne
Guernsey, 2009

ACKNOWLEDGEMENTS

My thanks to many friends and family: to Tony Ozanne, our rock; to Alison for consistent help, Caz Baudains, Nikki Travis and all at A O Hall. To Mike for his warm words, to Emily, Penny and Gordon Dawes (especially for his superb photograph of my father, Edwin Bréhaut on his beloved boat) for cheering Granny on. Thanks are due to Stephen Ainsworth and those at BWCI who launched *Love Apple Island* so successfully. Thanks to Di Digard, Features Editor and Richard Digard for their kind permission to reprint articles first published in their newspaper, the *Guernsey Press*, and for their unfailing help over the past ten years. Many thanks go to Roger Jones, of ELSP and Seaflower Books, for his meticulous editing and advice. Thanks to Robert Bréhaut of Alternative Solutions who, once more, eased me through daunting technicalities. My thanks to all the people who have contacted me with encouragement and advice, also to those establishments who have helped me with research.

A special thanks to Professor Edward Chaney for his kind words and for the interest he has shown in my writing. Similarly, thanks to Professor Godfrey Baldacchino and Guernsey States Minister Dave Jones. I am deeply indebted to you all.

Yvonne Ozanne
Guernsey 2009

1 Another Story

October 2007

The crunch of autumn is upon us. Every step we take tells us so. Out walking, leaves tumble down to join the mellow mulch that carpets the lane. Shiny red and yellow seeds, round as jewelled beads, split from dried flower casing. In the garden, gleaming orange-red hops and crimson berries are everywhere. Emerging mauve Michaelmas daisies lend colour to a landscape that knows full well winter beckons apace.

Purple veronica and lavender still bloom in quiet corners. Pastel pink, papery hydrangea will make pretty dried flower arrangements, now that their full glory is spent. We still have some fuchsias: the 'dancing ladies' of childhood.

Some escallonia leaves have turned yellow, yet in one or two places it still grows fragile pink blossoms. But, soon, the garden will draw itself in; the hedgerows begin their slow slumber and dig in their roots. Far down into the rich brown earth of St Pierre du Bois they burrow. The sun, fading for some time now, lowers so that driving westwards at dusk we have to pull down the sun visor so we are not dazzled by the powerful rays of the slowly setting orb.

For now, all is fruition. Seeds planted in spring have had their summer sun, their moisture and nutrition from the fertile soil. Autumn could be seen as a time of birth, when the natural cycle brings forth the fruit that has gestated for so long.

Now we have in abundance the apples, pears, blackberries and sloes to make our pies, chutneys and Christmas fare. Autumn brings with it colours that deny decay as long as possible: gold, nut-browns and vermilion. Pitted green leaves seem as beautiful, in their way, as the smooth, viridian green bay leaf. Dark green holly, spiky with confidence that it will grace our Christmas hall, also thrives. Yet ours has no red berries. We eye the next-door neighbours' splendid crop but won't take any and certainly not indoors until Christmas Eve, lest we bring ourselves bad luck.

Spiders' webs, strung carefully on the thorny rose bushes – the lovely June flowers have long gone – mass, intricately woven. I compare their circular shape to mushroom caps and prickly horse-chestnuts. Why is so much in nature circular? Yet, there is a pleasing rightness about round shapes: rotund and offering a kind of completeness.

Plump, also, are the rabbits: only babies a blink of an eye ago. They hop about fearlessly and, being no Mr McGregor, we cannot bring ourselves to chase them away. Baby birds, now almost grown, have fled their nests long ago and flit bossily around the treetops as though they own the place. Bees belatedly visit the *echium wildpretii*, but the wasps' days are numbered.

Yvonne aged six, 1948

Yvonne's drawing of Milly-Molly-Mandy

I loved the *Milly-Molly-Mandy* books when I was young because the author, Joyce Lancaster Brisley (1896-1978) illustrated the books herself and included a map of the lanes in the story. Milly-Molly-Mandy always wore the same striped dress, short white socks and white, elasticated knickers that showed just below her hem.

I would imagine myself as the story character, walking along the lane with a church in the distance and a village school. Milly-Molly-Mandy lived in a 'nice white cottage with a thatched roof' on a farm and she kept a duckling for a pet. She had her own vegetable patch and two friends who she 'camped' with under sheets and kitchen chairs.

In our Folie Lane we invariably met Mr Quevatre's large, meandering herd of Guernsey cows. What lovely creatures they were with their long faces and endearing brown eyes. Not quite as pretty as Jersey cows, maybe, but with their own, soulful charm.

At least, now, we can light our living room fires and make our autumnal bonfires, a most satisfying thing to do. Smoke billows as the fires crackle and hiss in the cool air.

Holiday brochures have been arriving through our letterbox for some time now. Holiday destinations seem to be getting further and further away. Holiday homes are offered in ever more foreign countries: Morocco, Croatia, Dubai… Goodness me, how far away does one need to go to relax?

Up St Andrews, that's where. St Andrews' fields and valleys are beautiful. There is a campsite that we want to try one day. We have only just discovered it. Walks around these valleys bring peace and quiet, open spaces and fresh air. You can even get there by bike. There is no need to take the car. What could be better than that?

Herm, Sark, Alderney and our very own Guernsey back gardens – these places all offer beauty and tranquillity. It is a matter of looking for them, to discover things – to stop and examine more closely. I read the *Press* article about Marguerite and Tony Talmage's wonderful vegetable and flower garden. They are neighbours and we greatly admire what they have achieved, with everything organic and of amazing variety. Hard work, yes, but immensely satisfying I'm sure.

The October night skies are black but sprinkled with a glitter of stars that seem shinier at this time of year. I try to look up at the sky now and then, as I walk. Clouds change shape and shade in seconds; a pale crescent moon can exist at the same time as the sun. Flocks of birds, some times in only twos or threes fly steadfastly and instinctively toward their homes. These creatures live alongside us yet we hardly notice them, so intent are we on dealing with road rage or letting an enormous vehicle squeeze past us, belching out fumes, on our walks.

There is still plenty of time before bitter cold bites, time before the real darkness of winter falls. As I write this, the sun is shining warmly. So, for now, we take the warmth offered and keep it deep in our hearts for when we might really need it. For ahead of us is November with its more fickle weather. We will get through it all though, like we do everything else.

2 Dressing Up

September 2003

Autumn Term: a time for new leather shoes, blackberrying and purple sloes waiting to be gathered. It is the end of the summer, but the beginning of a brand new year for school. Soon the polished new shoes will kick dry autumn leaves, gold and crinkled like cornflakes, into the gutters of the lane, as we walk to the school bus.

In the 1950s my new uniform, leather satchel, new pencils and gymkit are all ready for the Michaelmas season. The year has quietened down, the sand cooler now as we walk over the spike-grassed common on Saturday afternoons, salt sea spray on our faces. The lowering sun shades our rocks and cliffs, darker to lighter grey with dark fissures in their recesses. The little fields are patched straw yellow and dry green. The hedges and trees still have some leaves. In the autumn sun Herm and Sark stand clean against the sky. Alderney and the coast of France are more clearly defined.

In the greenhouses the tomato plants are pulled down, the packing shed is quiet. Now is the time for cleansing and repair before winter cold sets in. The workmen begin to wear their everyday navy Guernseys.

I remember my Southend uncle. He used to go to work in his office in London, in a pinstriped, three-piece suit and he wore a bowler hat. He had to go by train and took a rolled umbrella. I felt very sorry for him. My father could work out of doors, in just his shirtsleeves. He was always tanned brown by the end of the summer. His work was on our own land, outside our back door. We knew all the workmen by first name.

In the 1950s people wore hats. My great-uncle Alfred always wore a brown trilby. But, for my great-aunt Elise's funeral he wore a black top hat and full mourning dress. Although the war was over, our parents still wore a kind of uniform: black and grey or brown formal coats and hats even to places of leisure. "Should I wear a tie?" was never asked when they visited restaurants, because ties were always worn. Not that they made many visits to restaurants.

Two of my uncles and aunts always had the latest fashion. The men, both ex-RAF, were dark and handsome, their wives fair-haired and pretty.

They liked being fashionable, wearing the latest costumes, seamed stockings and Max Factor make-up. They were the first to have cars and television. Aunty Frances loved gold lamé and had a real fur stole. Uncle Edward had a thin moustache like Errol Flynn and sometimes wore a dinner jacket and bow tie. When they went out to the Nautique I thought they were the ultimate in sophistication.

Forest W.I. in Jersey, 1955. Tony's mother, Kath Ozanne, second from left

My father's first car was an old black Citroen with a running board so wide we could stand on it whilst he drove up the driveway. We used to call him Maigret when he had that car, because a television series about Simenon's French detective Maigret was very popular at that time and he had a Citroen. Like many of his friends Dad usually wore a sports jacket, grey flannels, white shirt and flat cap when going out informally.

Later he liked going to dinner-boxing and wore a dress shirt and evening dress. For my daughter's wedding in Oxford in 1989 he hadn't wanted to wear morning dress, with tails and grey topper. But someone mistook him for a Lord and after that we couldn't get him out of it.

Felt and straw hats with veils were popular for even quite young women.

17

Gloves and leather bags completed the ensemble. Even young girls wore berets, headscarves or pixie hoods. The boys wore caps, and not just for school. And they had short grey trousers, fair-isled jumpers and ties – even just for visits to the pictures.

On autumn Sundays we changed into Sunday best and after church went for walks around L'Ancresse and Pembroke. Many other families did the same. It was a social occasion. Instead of summer cotton frocks my mother wore a jacket, twin-sets and pleated skirts in the autumn.

People wore similar fashions: dressing differently was not the thing to do. There was no leisure wear, like tracksuits and trainers. That was sportswear. It would have been thought very common to wear things like that in Town or at the airport, and jogging was unheard of.

Delas, Coker, Mary Toms and Rabeys sold expensive goods of wool, tweeds, silk and leather. My mother-in-law wouldn't have dreamt of going anywhere else. She always dressed impeccably for visiting Town and taking tea at Le Noury's tearoom in the Arcade. Menswear was bought at Creighton's in the High Street, Creasey's, Amyson's and Keyho's. Gabriel's was best for school outfits, inexpensive and of good quality.

Even our doctor always wore a three-piece suit and his surgery was like a sitting-room. Nobody spoke in the waiting room and private visits to your own home were preferred. The family doctor was usually a man and someone you had known for years.

So the autumnal season has arrived: the flowers are fading, the hydrangeas losing their papery colour. Green leaves are mottling with yellow and gold. The berries are ripening. Memories are a bit like autumn. I remember how we bought new winter coats, woollen, warm and made to last.

The summer days of dancing, sunburn, wearing cotton tops, full flare skirts and three net petticoats are gone. And my father telling me off because my shoes were pink ("What on earth will people think of you?") is of quite another day.

We'll sit a little while yet in the sun, though, and toast those days of elegance and finery. Maybe an evening class awaits and all over the island school begins again. This is a new start – another time to enjoy a misty, mellow season in our beautiful island.

3 Herm, a paradise

August 2006

Herm was only three miles away, yet the 1940s' trips in open boats, like *Capwood* and *Maywood*, clutching a bag of crab sandwiches mum made, always felt adventurous and took ages. Sometimes the waves nearly came over the side and the boat swayed alarmingly. Adults, dressed in summer Sunday best, tried to look calm and sea-faring but I was never fooled. What if the boat capsized? At least I can swim, I thought, aged around six, gazing down at the wet green fathoms, wondering how long I could actually last before being rescued?

We would arrive at the harbour, clamber up the stone steps and head for Shell Beach. Belvoir bay came later, when we were in our teens and wanted to be seen somewhere which we thought more fashionable. Then, the more daring of us wore the new 'bikinis' and sunbathed in Herm's famous Gulf Stream waters. If you had a deep tan, people always asked "Have you been to Herm?"

In those 40s Shell Beach was pink and white with cowrie shells, pointed cream limpet and ormer shells with their mother-of-pearl lining. Hours were spent examining minute shells, some tinier than a little finger nail.

Then, it was into the sea for a dip, mindful of the often repeated warnings: "The sand shelves quickly. Don't go over your height!" And, once you were in, the cold sea both refreshed and energised. Then you ran up the beach to claim your towel and eat your sandwiches with a drink of Guppy's orange pop if you were lucky.

How long ago that seems. Last year I camped with my granddaughters at Herm's Seagull camping site. We loved it and will do it again. I have stayed at The White House Hotel.

But this year we went self-catering. The very first thing the children spotted was a swallow's nest, built in the corner of our kitchen window. Parent birds and babies' heads fearlessly peeped over the top.

What a revelation: we discovered not only a fabulous holiday experience, but a community. The little school with seven or so children hadn't broken up yet so we saw the Herm little ones enjoying their playtime and mum's

Herm, a paradise; view from the cottages to the harbour

Tony aged eleven, 1948

arriving, bearing flowers for the schoolteacher, on the last day of term.

Right next to our apartment, Sea Thrift, was St Tugual's church, superbly kept with fresh flowers at the altar. The peaceful little garden was amazing – planted with the purple, reds and blues of exotic flowers all set against lush green lawns. On the Sunday morning we heard the church bell, calling worshippers to a service held every week.

There is a humming generator, supplying the island with electricity. From The Keep, a castellated tower, a flag always flew, pointing toward the most sheltered bay. Alongside this was the Manor House and private gardens.

On our walks along Spine road, at the top of the island, we sketched. Once day we saw farmhands carefully relocating young calves from one field to the other. Two sweet dogs, Salty and Minty, sat happily in a box on the men's tractor. We learned that Herm has an important dairy farm and felt only slightly guilty when we ate Herm meat beefburgers (delicious!). We watched workmen mending fences and tending to the sleepy cattle. How wonderful for these animals to graze freely with the sparkling blue sea all around them with white gulls calling to each other in a cloudless sky.

We managed to be in Herm when a heat wave prevailed. As we gazed out of our window at the turquoise sea, dotted about with white yachts, listening to black and white oyster catchers with cheeky orange beaks, we felt we could be in the Caribbean. In the evenings it was warm enough to eat out and use the barbecue in the flowered courtyard.

How different it all felt from my young days when Herm seemed so far away and I worried what could happen to us, marooned as we were on this desert island. What if a storm came up? Whatever would we do if we couldn't get back to Guernsey?

Now, here I was, sleeping in Herm and looking out toward Guernsey. In the blue misty night, her coloured lights glistened along the coast and we never tired of this lovely sight.

Gradually the peace and beauty of Herm enveloped us. We felt part of the way of life. Everyone works very hard, looking after tourists, working the farm, serving food and drinks or helping at the Gift Shop.

I bought and read Jenny Wood's book, *Herm our Island Home*, and learnt of her and Major Peter Wood's incredible love of Herm and the enormous effort they put in to make Herm the gem it is today. And now Pennie, their daughter, and Adrian Heyworth, Pennie's husband (the

Woods' son-in-law), continue their wonderful work to keep the island as an undeniable paradise for us all to enjoy.

The donkeys and their rides on Herm have gone now, save for Katie, a good old girl with her own field and a notice not to feed her since her teeth aren't the best. But we saw free range chickens and pheasants and were charmed with the notice on the Herm school gate: 'Free Range Children. Please shut the gate.'

We walked accompanied by myriad butterflies and identified insects. On the way home the Travel Trident boatman pointed out a basking seal to us. It sprawled in the heat on a rock just off Jethou. We didn't want to leave.

The Wood family kept Herm safe for us. She is cherished and stunningly beautiful, like a flowery oasis in a blue-green, iridescent sea. The Wood family, then the Heyworths have achieved this not by acquiring the island for themselves, nor merely for financial gain. No, Herm still belongs to us: for the rich or for the less well off alike and for all those who want to spend time in the most heavenly place on earth.

Note: Since this article was published John and Julia Singer are new tenants of Herm. They are carrying on the good work magnificently.

4   A Lovesome Thing

July 2006

It is difficult to realise that gardens are now serious leisure areas. In the olden days, as my grandchildren call it, Guernsey growers never retired and, when they did, rarely sat about in their gardens. There was no such thing as a Garden Centre. Plants would be grown from seeds and cuttings. Men would have their own treasured penknife, a much valued tool, kept in their pocket for trimming off tomato shoots and cutting twine.

There were hobbies of course: boating, fishing and so on. But those who gardened mostly grew practical stuff like vegetables and fruit. Trust our tiny island, then, to have the oldest greenhouse in the British Isles where exotic flowers were and are still grown. Built in 1792 at Candie Gardens this elegant construction still delights us with the recent wonderful floral event held there.

Guernsey, for its size, holds remarkably many records covering several fields of endeavour. But, back to greenhouses and gardens. William Cowper wrote: 'Who loves a garden loves a greenhouse too.'

And T.E. Brown said: 'A garden is a lovesome thing, God wot!' (God knows).

So what is it that attracts us so to gardens, greenhouses, flowers and plants? Well, it all goes back a long way, probably to the Garden of Eden.

A certain kind of paradise is found in gardens, however small or grand. Earthly chaos has been tamed and changed to beautiful order. Last month we walked around the opened gardens of St Pierre du Bois. Proceeds went to the lost gardens of the parish church. How civilizing a thought that is. And how lovely the gardens were: uplifting and life-affirming.

One moment you were strolling over a baize of green lawn, edged with sweet-smelling, long-stemmed flowers with not a weed in sight. The next, you crossed narrow bridges and entered a dark green almost tropical jungle, cultivated but only just. Here, there were nettles for the butterflies; there a meandering sludge brown stream, home to the frogs and dragonflies.

Some gardens had seats for the weary to stop and admire the sunny fields and trees beyond. One or two gardens were formal, keeping to mathematical precision but none the less pretty for that. A few plots were so sprawling and wild that they could hardly be called gardens. So the owners had made walks for us to follow, real walks through rubbly paths and meadowland that took some effort. But all the while the scent of blooms and lushness of the scenery made our attempts worthwhile.

My love of gardens began with my Great Uncle Alfred and his gardening skills. This was his hobby as well as his living and he grew cabbages, onions, potatoes and soft fruit. His favourite flowers were flimsy pink dog roses, lilacs that he warned were poisonous and geraniums, especially the traditional red. The scent and colour of these plants always make me think of him. And Uncle Alfred had a lean-to conservatory built to the side of his house, where he tended his favourites and showed us how to set them off to best advantage with clay flower pots of all sizes inverted one on top of the other.

For a treat Uncle Alf would take his sister Elise, my brother and me for an afternoon-long taxi tour of prize-winning gardens. I loved the Guernsey houses that mostly went with them in those days – the late 40s. The graceful Vale houses always seemed to be cream-coloured with peaceful windows, set back and reflecting the afternoon sun. We would crunch over gravel paths and admire flowerbeds and Uncle Alfred would talk knowledgeably to the proud owners.

Our own first house had a very modest garden which we laid to lawn. On one side we planted tall orange calendula at the back, night stock and starry white allysium on the borders. In the evening we walked around, breathing in the night stock scent as if we were landowners of some acres. Bright yellow and deep red nasturtiums soon spread alarmingly over a rock garden we made in the front and they quickly dominated that small square.

Then our two children began to play in the garden so it rapidly turned into a plot of grass with swings and a place to kick a ball, rather than a place to admire any gardening efforts. Alison loved her toy telephone and hasn't stopped talking since, albeit now on her beloved 'Blackberry'. In his swing, Michael's feet didn't touch the ground. Some things never change, then.

Later, we discovered that Tony had a real way with roses. Gorgeously scented – cream with pink edges; pink and white stripes and all shades of red and crimson always delight.

Alison aged two and Michael aged six months at The Lee, our first little garden, 1968

Soon we will attend a charity function in friends' superb garden. It is beautifully landscaped on different levels with some delightful hidden surprises waiting to be discovered. Again, friends held a garden lunch. Their house is a stone's throw from where I grew up, opposite the Vale pond and meadow. It was delightful eating good food in good company, recalling the live acts we used to be able to see and enjoy at St George's Hall and Candie Gardens. We bird-spotted whilst admiring the handiwork of our hosts. You could hear the bells of the Vale church from where we sat.

"Stands the Church clock at ten to three?

And is there honey still for tea?"

Well, no, maybe not quite Rupert Brooke's idyll, but close. Maybe that's it: the timeless quality of being in a flower-filled garden on a sunny day. Hearing the parish church bells brings back memories unsullied by worries. Don't we all like pottering about in greenhouses, however amateur we are and even if it is made of aluminium now, not traditional wood? Still it is exciting to see green shoots appearing. We might even manage real red tomatoes that we can claim to be organic.

Perhaps a garden, then, is paradise after all: a place where we can all go to and find beauty and peace and a well earned rest from everyday stress, just for once.

5 Christmas Stars

December 2007

I have always loved the glitter of Christmas time: the lights and decorations on people's houses, in shops and restaurant windows. It must be something primordial, mustn't it? For something that is shining, glowing bright and alive is full of warm promise. How very apt, then, gleaming gold and silver, red and green, shimmer and shine in the very depths of a dark, icy cold December.

As a child, wrapped warmly in a knitted woolly scarf, made by my mother, I would sit on Aunt Elise's cushioned seat and gaze out of the winter window. The darkening sky tipped crystal drops on to the clear windowpane: rain. So the winter scene outside, of a chilly, wet meadow and de-leafed trees could be seen, but only through a translucent screen of raindrops.

Damp, yellowed leaves skittered across our gravelled garden path as though to seek shelter under the icy hedge, shadowed blue with cold. Yes, December is here again. Yet December also brings Advent, with the promise of something special about to happen. Although the Christingle (Christ light) celebration is fairly new, it tells an old message. A round orange (representing the world, tied with red ribbon, symbolising Christ's suffering) pierced with four spears that represent the four seasons and embellished with small fruit and sweets (denoting recreation) children can carry the lit Christingle candle with both safety and excitement. There are four Christingle candles: Hope, Peace, Joy and Love. These are all very human needs, all existing since time began.

Here in December once more, are the Pantomimes and Christmas plays that give us the chance to step outside of everyday life and into a world where tinsel stars, starry crowns and sparkling rods become real diamonds and magic wands. Maybe we could all do with a fairy godmother to make our dreams come true.

Little children act out the timeless Nativity scene. The newly born baby Jesus is safe in his warm, straw cradle. His family, Mary and Joseph (highly prized roles) lovingly tend to Him.

At Christmas, when we were teenagers, we went to parties and dances in hotels. We girls, in taffeta skirts and shoes with unaccustomed high heels – hair sticky with spray from a plastic puffer – showed off our *diamanté* jewellery. Dresses were lace, brocade and soft velvets in the deep colours of ruby red, royal blue and emerald green and gold: the jewel colours. I still find the twinkling lights on green fir trees, probably decorated with the hotel staff, somehow even more spectacularly glamorous than those at home.

In my youth, it would be unusual for adults to take any more time off than Christmas Day and Boxing Day, not the two (or even more) weeks that some people take now. For me, it was a special time because we had our parents to ourselves. Just for once they weren't out in the greenhouses, fields or fishing way out at sea. They were indoors, anticipating Christmas fare with their family and friends. There was a feeling of plenty and worries were forgotten – just for a short while.

Families come together at Christmas and New Year as at no other time of the year. As we grow older we recognise how transient life can be: it is impermanent. Like snow, however beautiful, happiness can vanish and like a sparkling, crisp frost, it can thaw as suddenly as it first appeared. As a little girl I loved the words of a particular carol. The words are repeated over and over, just like the softly falling drift of snowflakes:

> 'Snow had fallen, snow on snow,
> Snow on snow.
> In the bleak mid-winter, long, long ago.'

This year manufacturers are producing a range of wooden toys. You can now buy wooden go-karts, Noah's arks, train sets and bird boxes. This, say those following market trends, is because people have begun to recognize once more the value of handing toys down to other generations. Yes, the wooden building blocks and farmyard sets, dolls house and garages are returning. Apparently children are becoming bored with primary coloured plastic things and are binning them unceremoniously without a second thought. Well then, we wondered just how long that was going to take, didn't we?

It is important for us to retain our childhood memories and well-loved toys, of warm gatherings and of happy times. We show our love for each other with prettily wrapped presents and we send invitations for others to

Tony's mother Kath (then Carré) as Cinderella, 1913. Note pumpkin and mice

share our homes. We send cards and donations to favourite charities. This year, I especially think of the homeless. Yes, even in 'idyllic' Guernsey there are people without a loving family or cheering fireside: no room at the inn.

By the time you read this, the winter solstice – the sun (sol) standing still (stice) – on 22nd December will be about to happen. From now on the sun will slowly return to us, a minute each day so that, by spring, around March in Guernsey, we can be warmed again by balmy sunlight. Dawn light will come earlier and last a little longer in the evening. The dark green spears, the leaves of daffodil bulbs that have braved the recent howling gales and freezing cold, can already be seen.

We all need light at the end of our personal tunnels, something to aim for. Especially those, who, perhaps, have endured just a little more than their fair share of pain or loss this year. Like the solstice, the bright star of Bethlehem symbolises the light of hope – a star standing still in a darkened sky – marking the place that shows the end of a journey and the beginning of Jesus' birth as the Light of the World. Never mind that Christianity really began in a land of sandy desert and palm trees and certainly no snow at all. As with all leaps of faith, Christians of the Western world have taken the story of Christmas to their hearts and understood its promise: a true light in the winter darkness.

I wish you all a very Happy Christmas and a peaceful New Year.

6 Firelight

"Are you sitting comfortably? Then I'll begin..." But this question has to be asked in front of a roaring fire, doesn't it? The 'roaring' will be preferably, of logs crackling and merrily thrusting out tongues of orange and yellow flame. The room will be quiet save for a winter wind whistling outside whilst we toast ourselves so warmly we almost doze off.

Ah, the fireside. The cleaning out of the ashes of a morning, the sweeping up of coal dust with a little brass brush from the companion set; then, with the tongs we select pieces of coal to put on top of the kindling already catching the draught and burning the newspaper so that, once more, a fire is lit.

As the story was read to us we used to gaze into the fire, much as we do at television nowadays. Amongst the black soot tiny sparkling orange-red stars shot up the chimney. As a child I thought it looked like some kind of magic kingdom: coal-black caves lit within and changing all the while with each thundering crack of the fuel, sending up showers of crimson dust.

The fireplace was the focal point of the room. It still can be, even if it is now a redundant feature, left as a mere frame, with a mantelpiece for our photographs, clocks and candlesticks. Time was, the easy chairs were grouped around the fireplace, whilst the colder parts of the room were reserved for bookcases, sideboards and nests of tables. A hearthrug was really that, a rug in front of the hearth, upon which lucky cats and dogs stretched themselves out, letting the fire's heat warm their bones.

My great Uncle Alfred didn't allow the fire to be lit until four o clock every day. But, then, he and my Great Aunts had lived through the Occupation and knew a frugal thing or two. So Aunt Elise would entertain guests around four, with tea and cakes as her cats hid under the brown chenille covered table, peeping at the fire with covetous eyes, waiting for everyone to go away so that they could reclaim their territory.

We didn't have time for such things. Both my parents worked in the greenhouses, the packing shed and with their carting business: collecting other people's tomatoes for store packing, and yes, doing coal deliveries

Granny Lenfesty, 1950

Great Aunt Belle in her Hauteville Town House, 1936

as well – anthracite for the growers' boilers which had to be de-clinkered, stoked and fed every day, seven days a week in season.

Most times, when we lit our fire, my mother would use it to air clothes, especially in the winter. We had a fireguard which regularly held baby clothes, towels and socks. Before the days of washing machines and tumble dryers, women's lives were ruled by the weather and washing was an exhausting, major chore. Eventually a boiler room was made for my mother in an outhouse but this was also run on coal and both the lighting of it and maintaining a decent furnace was a nightmare.

Over these Christmas holidays I decided to do something I hadn't done for many years. I decided to light our fire and sit by it all afternoon with a book. This was a special treat and absolute heaven. During one of the bad storms a year ago, our old, dead, elm tree fell across our driveway. We had it cut into logs and stored them.

As I threw more elm logs onto the fire they spat sparks and the brown bark began to roast, all glowing red ridges underneath. I poked the fire with great satisfaction as shards glimmered hotly in the grate. Then I went back to my book until suppertime feeling utterly relaxed and cosy.

It later dawned on me that this 'special treat' had once been a daily occurrence of no particular note in thousands of households. Fires were lit in town and country without a second thought. But what comfort they brought with them, and what a feeling of being curled up, safe in one's own home.

A town house, elegant with its drawing room fire, would have been such a civilised place to be in. In the Guernsey country houses, some fireplaces were big enough to sit in, preferably with a glass of something soothing.

I like to remember how Guernsey people, outside of St Peter Port and the more residential areas, used to brave the outdoor elements, with no street lighting, buses or transport, save horse and carriage. One time my pregnant daughter and I – walking the deserted lanes of St Pierre du Bois – got caught in a snowstorm. We pushed the buggy with the sleeping toddler, wrapped in woollen hat and mittens. As we scurried through the snow flurry, the flakes sticking to our coats, we imagined how it would have been in the wilder 'olden days', with country people wearing long black capes, heads down, wending homeward. And I imagine them walking on our blustery cliffs, feeding cows and horses, then hurrying home to a waiting fireside and the promise of a hearty meal cooking slowly with succulent aromas in vast Guernsey kitchens.

But then, these, of course, are memories and we have central heating now throughout our houses: even in bedrooms, bathrooms and all. Still, as January has a week or so left before we can say it is, at least, early spring; maybe we can light a fire once again and sit beside it. Hopefully, someone might keep us company with a story or two as we look to our future and the brighter days to come.

7 Family Roots

March 2008

Just before force ten gales rattled over the cliffs, shores and lanes of our fair island we had felled a towering *Leylandii* tree. Apart from casting too long a shadow, the tree had become potentially dangerous, easily blown down to damage our cottage roof. So we were relieved that the tree had been removed before high force winds whistled all around us. So far, all well and good. Trouble is that there are now some very puzzled looking birds sitting in the opposite sycamore trees, wondering where their nests have gone.

I hadn't liked to ask the tree-feller fellows if they had found nests, I didn't really want to know the sad truth. Also, I can imagine how the birds might be feeling. Good husbandry may mean culling but branches get lost and cause disorientation. Attempting to trace our Irish family tree, we have discovered many important gaps where records are obscure.

We are slowly getting there, but mass migration from troubled lands can cause such a separation of people from their original roots. Think of our evacuation from the island during the Second World War and all the disruption that caused.

But, usually, most Guernsey people are fortunate because we have many excellent places of reference when we want to trace our family trees. Long living families, friends and neighbours often have vivid recollection of who was who, where people lived and when they died.

Older folk often have excellent memories and can recall valuable facts just in the telling of their individual stories. In the old days such a thing as the nuclear family unit existed, in fact it was imperative for community strength. Although this may be difficult to find now in some countries, it is still not extinct in Guernsey.

The month of March includes Mothering Sunday in its calendar, but my mother Mary Bréhaut was recently pleased to be made a great-great-grandmother with the February arrival of Ethan James. There is always cause for a special celebration for a new baby – another generation is born, promising both a continuation and a future. I am not sure how pleased I am to be made a great-great-aunt but that is another subject entirely.

In the photograph, taken in 1907, my husband, Tony's family of the Carrés, Symons and Batistes are grouped together. Great, great-grandmother Rouly (with immaculate white hair) is resplendent in her elegant best. Her daughter, great-grandmother Anne Louise Carré (nee Batiste) sits alongside her and behind them is Tony's grandmother, Isabella Carré, nee Symons. Sitting right in the front in a white outfit, holding a bucket and spade, is Tony's mother, Kath Carré who, when in her twenties, married Claude Ozanne. Alongside Kath is her sister Isabel. Their brother James (Bustie) Carré was yet to be born.

Four generations of the Carré family, 1907

The Carré family lived at 39 Hauteville, St Peter Port, moving later to a cottage at Petit Bôt. Their photographs, kept in albums and carefully dated, show an enviably stylish life and close-knit relationships.

Nowadays, as young people move to follow their employment, some to countries hundreds of miles from their home town, friends might become their 'family'. Instead of mothers and sisters, aunts and grandmothers, women, especially, can form sympathetic and deep bonds which can be very sisterly indeed. Older women – easier and less competitive – may become surrogate mums. For a mother whose own daughter may have flown far from the nest, these young women are, in return, welcome company.

Easter fast approaches with more new beginnings, eggs and nests, and we islanders have witnessed many changes. Easter is a time of re-generation and renewal, yes, but sometimes change is so rapid that it overtakes us almost without our noticing.

I recently attended a wonderful lecture on Venice, its artists and poets at St James Concert Hall. At the dinner afterward I spoke to fellow art lovers. It turned out that I was the only Guernsey person on my table. It isn't that one minds so much – we cannot survive without the Open Market and licence holders' money entering our economy. They are a vital part of our continuing to be successful within a global market. It's just that there is a sense of loss when you cannot share memories of, after all, not so very long ago. For example, nobody knew what importance a love-apple was to us nor could quite share what impact the tomato had had on us Guerns. Nobody knew about packing sheds and stoking boilers. It made me go very quiet, I can tell you – not an easily produced phenomenon, as my friends will readily verify.

Sitting there, in a beautifully decorated room, with columns delightfully bedecked with ribbons, I recalled St James itself when it was a church, used by Elizabeth College boys for their morning service. When the hall was the venue for bring and buy sales. When Kath Carré grew up she was instrumental in the organising of St James Christmas and Easter bazaars. That, of course, was all in her future. How very quickly those years have become the past. It's a bit like losing relatives and felling trees: one minute they are there, living and thriving and the next they have gone.

Never mind. Nothing stays the same forever. The sun streams through my kitchen window now whereas before it was blocked out by the dark, evergreen needles of *Leylandii*. You can see right over to the hedgerows and meadow, as well as our neighbour's geese. So, perhaps then, a different view and a bit of clearing out of dead wood is no bad thing after all?

8 Ebenezer: Stone of help

August 2009

Ebenezer Le Page, now there's a name we've all heard of. Ebenezer means 'Stone of Help'. The word comes from the Hebrew for stone, *even*, and help, *ezer*. Although the 'stone of hope' is also referred to. The Bible tells us that Samuel set up a marker-stone, naming it the stone of help (*Ebenezer*) to commemorate God's support of the Israelites' victorious battle over the Philistines when they regained the stolen Ark of the Covenant (a most Holy part of the Hebrew Tabernacle). An *Ebenezer* is not only a stone, but can be any representation of faith, such as a cross.

Gerald Basil Edwards, who wrote *Ebenezer Le Page*, produced a funny and moving book but it is also very learned, albeit written lightly. Though Ebenezer mentions people like Mozart, Shakespeare, the Bible and a couple of other classics, Edwards reveals a cultured and knowledgeable mind. He was far more educated than his creation, Ebenezer, though Ebenezer was a wise, canny old bird who can mean a lot by saying very little. Edwards calls this the Guernsey 'quirky, tragic-comic, down-to-earth humour' that we certainly recognize.

Edwards, like Victor Hugo, writes about our island as a beautiful granite rock, surrounded by many other rocks and islands. *Pierre* means rock . St Peter Port and St Pierre du Bois are named after St Peter; "this is the rock upon which I build my church," said Jesus. Think of the names we have chosen for our island and you can see how they dominate us: *Perelle* (bay of rocks); *Piette* (rocky coast); *Hougue à la Père* (mound on rocky shore); *Icart* (rocky headland). Then there are *Rocquaine* (rocky seashore) and *La Rochelle* (small rock) to name just a few. I am sure you can add to the list: *Rocquettes, Grand Rocques*, White Rock.

Our lighthouses testify to the dangerous rocks surrounding us: the Casquets and the treacherous coast where the Hanois gives light to the sailors. Think of all the wrecks we used to have around the west coast. Even now there are parts of Guernsey's craggy coast where only the most knowledgeable of sea-goers may negotiate. Even the everyday trips

G B Edwards (seated) author of Ebenezer Le Page

we take without thinking of danger, to Herm and Sark, are not without hazard to any but the experienced.

Where I live now, Mount Hermon in St Peter Port, two tall spires grace the sky. St Joseph's, built of Guernsey blue granite, and Ebenezer in Brock Road. What a pity the Brock Road church is to be demolished. The two religions, Roman Catholic and Methodist, are constant themes for Edwards. In his story he writes of Ebenezer saying Guernsey was originally Christianised by Celtic saints. However, he himself 'if Christianised at all, was by the spiritual descendants of John Wesley [Methodism]'. He constantly compares Church and Chapel. It is also interesting that Edwards has Ebenezer telling the character, Raymond, that the moral of Robinson Crusoe is that it is foolish to go gallivanting around the world when you could stay at home leading a quiet life. This is such a true way of Guernsey thinking. My father liked saying, when asked where he was going on holiday, "I'm going to Romania" (remain 'ere), meaning Guernsey was good enough for him, he didn't need any fancy, foreign place for his holidays.

L'Ancresse. Note absence of sea wall

Indeed, how many times have we gone on holiday, only to return with relief to this island? Just back from Provence, we went to St Tropez, a busy, cosmopolitan resort. The harbour was teeming with millionaire, possibly billionaire, yachts. Simon Cowell's sailed in the day we were there. Yet, we said smugly, St Tropez isn't a patch on St Peter Port harbour. When we dine on our wonderful seafood on the seafront and the tide is high, reflecting the dazzling lights of town. Well, yes, that is quite unbeatable.

Guernsey rock once formed an important, vital, foundation of the Guernsey economy, giving much needed employment. The days when quarrying was king – the days of the 'stone rush' when the quarries of the North were opened, was a hard but lucrative life. Especially, of course, for the quarry owners. Granite was exported to London where its Embankments and steps of St Paul's Cathedral bear witness to its durability. Along the former Doyle's Military Road (Route Militaire) are quarrymen's cottages. The skills needed to mine, cut and hone the granite were varied and highly valued. From this industry came stonemasons and builders. The Victor Hugo statue in Candie Gardens needed huge blocks of granite. The carrying of these, by horse power, all the way to St Peter Port and then up the hill was a monumental task in itself.

There is a history here that I will write of another day. Meantime Edwards makes us laugh as Ebenezer remarks what a pity Queen Victoria (her statue is also in Candie) had to spend her time looking at the backside of Hugo. However, the building of what is now the Guernsey Museum at least saved her that sight.

Edwards had planned several more stories, one of which he was going to entitle *La Rocque Qui Chante: songs of a Guernseyman*. 'The Rock That Sings' – what an enchanting thought. Talking of a Guernsey identity and culture, Edwards quotes from a biblical idea: Isaiah 'Look unto the rock whence you are hewn'. Our Guernsey blue granite is a symbol of perpetuity. Lasting forever.

Victor Hugo's *Toilers of the Sea* is dedicated to the people of Guernsey: 'this rock of hospitality and liberty, that corner of old Norman soil where dwells that noble little people of the sea...'

Homofaber sums up the Guernsey spirit: man the builder and victor in his struggle with and against the forces of nature. *Ebenezer Le Page* is a profound story of his loves: Guernsey and Liza Queripel. Yet, the strong friendships he has – with Jim Mahy, Raymond and Horace, Neville Falla (to whom he leaves his book and all his money) – are touching and superbly drawn.

More of *Ebenezer Le Page* and Gerard Basil Edwards next time. *A la perchoin*.

9 Guernsey born: G.B. Edwards and the Heaumes

August 2009

Gerald Basil Edwards was born in Guernsey at Sous les Hougues, on July 8th in 1899. His father was Tom Edwards, a quarryman and his mother, Charlotte, was a Mauger. When Edwards was one the family moved to Hawkesbury House, Braye Road, Vale. There he lived until he was seventeen.

In 2008 Professor Edward Chaney, to whom Edwards dedicated *Ebenezer Le Page* and who holds the copyright for the book, unveiled with Jane Mosse, a Blue Plaque at Hawkesbury House to commemorate Guernsey's celebrated author. When I learned that G.B. Edwards had lived so close to our, Heaume, family home – Solidor, Route Militaire, Vale – I became intrigued. It occurred to me that the Heaumes might well have known Edwards and he, them. Indeed, in the 1800s the Braye Road and what was then Doyle's Military Road had far less housing and traffic than now. Even within my own memory there were still meadows and open fields all around. The house opposite Hawkesbury House (formerly owned by the Stafford-Allen family) included land that could be seen from Solidor, also from my great-aunt's property – now the Vale Church Rectory. It is not inconceivable, then, that walking and passing by with pony and trap they would have, at least, greeted each other.

There are several other interesting details: my great-aunt, Louise Dorey was a Heaume – a sister of the relations we were brought up with. Louise made her home with Alfred Dorey and they lived at Summerfield Road, Sous les Hougues. Great-aunt Elise (born 1887) and great-uncle Alfred (born 1890), Louise Heaume, Lilian and Nicholas were all brought up in Solidor.

But before that the Heaumes lived at Le Hougue and La Grève, Vale, places G.B. Edwards would have known well. By the descriptions in *Ebenezer* he was very familiar with the lanes and the whole area in Braye du Valle where the Domailles (the maiden name of the Heaumes' mother) lived. The Domailles are a large family and owned a lot of land and property all around the Vale Church, L'Ancresse, Chouet and as far as Les Mares Pellées, just off the Braye Road.

As I delved more into researching a connection with the Solidor family and G.B. Edwards I re-read *Ebenezer Le Page* and became fascinated by the book, seeing it in a different light than from my first reading. 'Ebenezer' himself says he is no scholar, but Edwards' own education comes through continually, albeit very subtly. Ebenezer talks about theology and the Bible in detail, also politics: "Guernsey is becoming a totalitarian state…" He mentions Hitler, Cromwell, and the Saracens. Ebenezer shows his knowledge of the Lukis Museum, the Ancient Monuments Committee and Société Guernesiaise. He loves Beethoven's *Pathetique* and *Voluntary* and says Mozart is 'like clear water, singing'. He knows the works of Bernard Shaw, Dickens and, especially, *Robinson Crusoe* by Daniel Defoe. Edwards/Ebenezer particularly likens the Crusoe story to his own. 'Ebenezer' is familiar with Cezanne's *Mont Victoire* paintings and knows the significance of *The Light of the World*.

Although the character Ebenezer can be very 'Guernsey' with his tongue firmly in his cheek, during the Occupation of Guernsey by the Germans 'the stolid, literal German mind was no match for the Guernsey wink…'. Ebenezer talks with a great sensitivity about nature and the human condition.

As Professor Chaney puts it, Edwards demonstrates what Renaissance Italians called *sprezzatura* – the art of achieving something difficult without apparent effort. And, as Edwards says, accused of writing a somewhat sentimental ending for *Ebenezer* – 'Romantic is not a dirty word.'.

The wry insights make you smile: " 'Guernsey has been improving for the worse these last years, even me, who have lived here all my life, can hardly recognise it.' 'My parents didn't speak much. My mother would say 'Will you do that?' My father would say 'Yes'. My father would say 'Can I do this?' My mother would say 'No.' "

There are some beautiful passages: 'I have lived all my days to the sound of the bells of the Vale Church, coming to me on the wind over the water.' And (at 'Raymond's' first and last attempt at holding a service) sitting outside on the grass, listening, under a sky clear as pearl, there was 'the likes of the seaman, who was singing like the roaring of the sea.' 'This island, down the years, has been a singing rock.'

On romance, Ebenezer's great love, Liza Queripel, says, 'They was

Louise, Elise and Alfred Heaume, c. 1893

lovers. They was mad.' Then, he is quite lyrical about 'Neville Falla', the friend he leaves his money, book and property to: 'It is his laugh saves him. It warms the world.'

It is debated whether G.B. Edwards based *Ebenezer* on his own life. Although there are always bound to be some biographical details in any book, I think Edwards is most like the character Raymond, a romantic, somewhat lost soul. Raymond was 'a Guernsey boy, first to last'. This reflects Edwards' true love of Guernsey, although in self-imposed exile. Incidentally, Professor Chaney told me that the Weymouth house in which Edwards ended up as a lodger is very like Solidor.

If you haven't already, I urge you to read *Ebenezer Le Page*. It will make you laugh out loud and weep silently. When Ebenezer says with all his heart, "When I think of what has happened to our island, I could sit down on the ground and cry," I wonder what the Heaumes and indeed all of our ancestors would say if they could see us now?

'It is an island of ghosts and strangers,' says Ebenezer. Well, not quite. I prefer to think of Guernsey as an island of spirits. Our family spots at chosen bays are never strange to us. Nor are the places of granite rock, the blue-green sea and sweet meadows. Nor are our memories of houses and lives built by our forbears faded. Long after man has made his money, stayed or gone away, Guernsey will remain forever.

10 Sweet Chariots

October 2005

'A Charabanc', I read, 'is from the French a *Char a banc* – a 'chariot with seats'. What fun it would be if charabancs still existed. How nice to be transported around our lovely island in a 'chariot with seats'.

I look forward to my bus pass in a few years' time and will use it with much enthusiasm. Just imagine: no driving. No looking for a parking place – no fine if I am delayed, strolling around Town with its colourful flags and pretty flower boxes. Or gazing at the myriad yachts, with flags from all countries as they float on our deep and shining sea.

No, on a bus I shall sit back and look at the well-kept gardens of our islanders and let the driver deal with today's driving horrors. Things like huge motors – the width and height of coaches – pulling out of yellow lines in front, just as we were about to pass by. Pedestrians stroll across the road looking neither left nor right. Cyclists cycle in twos – causing tailbacks of increasingly frustrated drivers.

Road rage, and too many cars on our roads and lanes, have ruined driving for me. No, I cannot wait to visit Rocquaine and L'Ancresse by bus. And I shall take some of the tourist trails – join the visitors in a cup of tea and a piece of gâche at one of our delightful cafés, in serenity and peace of mind. I can even partake in a glass of wine! Or two! Bliss!

Buses have always been used for treats. Even the Royal Family use them for their weddings – bussing whole parties to the church and reception. Yes, buses are fun. Buses took us on Sunday School outings, the pictures (remember the picture bus?) and once we hired one for a New Year's Eve so that everyone could enjoy themselves.

Yes, there is something different about sitting in a bus and being taken somewhere. Years ago the Paragons (blue) took us north. The Guernsey Motors were red and the Guernsey Railway was green. There were the Greys (Watsons) which serviced St Peter's and you could go to Pleinmont in them. Later, there was Sarre Transport (orange) for Torteval.

Roads were, if not empty, clearer – like Normandy and Brittany are – so that driving is still pleasant there. I recall being four years old and

Family outing, 1928

*Tony with his mother Kath
(née Carré) Ozanne, 1938*

standing at a bus stop with my mother outside our house. We could see the bus coming, heading toward L'Ancresse. There was no other traffic going either way – this on the Route Militaire. But I wouldn't get on, because I thought the bus had an ugly face. The windows looked like sad eyes and a bit in front stood out like a nose. Nothing my mother could say to me would change my mind. I think we walked to L'Ancresse that day.

And what about trams? The tramlines from the Bridge to St Peter Port still exist. What a good idea it would be if someone dug them up again. Commuters could read the *Guernsey Evening Press* as they travelled to and from the finance sector. A tram would deliver them fresh and happy to start their day. No rushing to the North Beach at eight o'clock in the morning, ready to kill for a parking place. Now, wouldn't that be nice?

I have travelled by tram in Blackpool – a resort that I am fond of. There is something quite exotic about hearing the bell being clanged as the tram approaches. When you are in Blackpool you feel immediately at home once you've shared a seat with a fellow passenger.

In the picture, the charabanc doesn't have pneumatic tyres, just solid rubber, and the road looks as though it had not been tarred. But Charabancs were built and made for people to enjoy and share their journey.

People sing in charabancs – things like *Ten Green Bottles* – and they wave at everyone passing by. People wave back. Imagine that – singing if you were on a train, or indeed, an aeroplane? Or the London Underground? Or the Herm ferry? Perhaps we should try it.

The more that our roads are used the grumpier we have become. We sit in our individual metal machines and concentrate on negotiating the filter systems; the traffic lights; the roundabout at the bottom of St Julian's Avenue – and the vexing one at Ville au Roi. We glare at each other if one small move is wrong.

We fight for parking places and drive round and round the piers – ever more crossly shouting at old ladies to get a move on as they load their shopping in the boot. We want the space and we want it now. How angry we are when we see people using disabled and parent/toddler spaces when they obviously are not entitled to them. Driving cars makes us impatient, anxious and judgemental.

No, much more delightful to alight at the Bus Terminus for a day's enjoyment of Town. I won't be able to buy too much because of the weight of the shopping bag. But there will be something very precious gained: time.

Time to listen to people's chatter and to meet friends. Time to visit Guille-Alles Library and pop into the Castle Cornet exhibitions. To stroll around Candie Gardens and see the Museum there and then the nearby Priaulx library for a mooch round its wonderful treasures. And then, another bus trip and I could be at the Cup and Saucer museum and still with time for another cup of tea.

Ahhh…buses – 'Chariots with Seats'. Transport me for free. Can't wait.

11   Diamond Days

February 2009

"Diamonds are forever," "Diamonds are a girl's best friend".

In the 1950s almost everyone got engaged. We'd gaze into the windows of the jewellery shops in the Arcade. Maybe a solitaire diamond ring? Or a cluster, or a sapphire with diamonds? Also, it was fashionable in those days to have a white gold band with diamonds, then later a wedding ring to match. A few years after marriage, possibly with the arrival of a first baby, you could expect an Eternity Ring to complete the set.

Some girls had more than one engagement but never gave the rings back. *Diamanté* jewellery was all the rage then – and my sister was once given a lovely *diamanté* bracelet for Valentine's Day. I was very envious.

Not so many pierced ears when we were young and dangly earrings were mostly for evenings. We went to dances wearing dolman sleeved tops with a V-neck, full skirts with waists cinched in tight as you could. How exciting it was in the 1950s, to jive and do the rock and roll to Elvis Presley's *Hound Dog* and Buddy Holly's *Peggy Sue* and *That'll be the Day*. Music like theirs broke the mould of romantic ballads and big bands. The dance floor was never the same again and we newly named 'teenagers' were heady with the brand new American style.

Still, sparkling sequins were rarely worn in the day time. They were more for the winter dances and New Year's Eve. Even then for evening only, perhaps Christmas Day being an exception. Nowadays, of course, people wear pretty sequined clothes summer or winter, day or evening.

It took some time for it to be thought normal for men to wear bright colours, to go tie-less and to wear items like shorts whenever they felt like it. Now men have the freedom to wear light coloured shoes, cropped cotton trousers, in fact almost anything they want to. Make up, beauty products and jewellery for men were thought quite outrageous and hardly existed.

Women have gained more freedom, too. Take this 1950s advertisement for Amami wave set lotion: 'Clever wives, wanting their husbands' admiration, have a quick set with Amami. Never an off-looking moment!"

Articles in women's magazines said things like: 'Business trips and entertaining VIPs should all be accepted as part of wife-manship. That is if you want your husband's promotion!' And 'At 30 a woman conducts herself with elegance and maintains a home that is remarkable for its serenity and vivacity...'

No grey areas there, then. A woman's place was in the home catering for her husband and she was expected to do all the housework. She had to be seen as a woman for whom a man could show off as his perfect wife, cook, cum domestic organizer.

Left to right: Peter Ozanne, Margaret Ozanne, John Ozanne, Mary Hardwick, Susan Vaudin, Peter Cox, Barry Vaudin, Claire Cox, Yvonne Ozanne, Tony Ozanne, Mike Green, Kate Green, 1961

But, in the last thirty years or so, gender roles have radically changed. As women have gradually eased away from the 'master-slave' marriage and sought their own professions a quite different set of problems are facing them. Whilst they found alternative lives, so have the men. Now that men do not have to marry, exchange rings or bring up their children they can find commitment a difficult thing to achieve. Men and women are no longer expected to 'put up' with each other for the sake of society and any children they have.

Bonding with someone and binding with someone are not now necessarily intertwined. This change has not always brought the happiness either sex sought. In simpler days, when society told you what to do, you conformed. Those who did not had a tough time of it. My father expected his home-cooked, dinner on the table whenever he stopped work to eat. In turn, my mother expected my father to provide for us all and for housekeeping money each week. They both worked long hours in the greenhouses and packing sheds. All those of that generation in Guernsey did so.

To illustrate the times, here is a wonderful, very old Guernseyman joke I was told recently:

A man went into the *Guernsey Press* to place a death notice.

"Mrs Gallichan has died," it said.

"Oh," said the girl at the desk, "Don't you want to say more?"

"No," said Mr Gallichan. "I'm a grower and my bottom bunch was no good this year."

The girl went off to find the manager and he came back with her. "Look, Mr Gallichan", he said, "I understand your predicament. May I, as a gesture of goodwill, offer you four more words for free?"

"Oh, alright, then," said Mr Gallichan, having a think. Then he replied, "Mrs Gallichan has died. Ladies bicycle for sale."

Today, when so much is ready prepared, the majority of women work outside the home in all sectors and levels of the community. Everyone travels more (though the recession may yet change that) and are more demanding. Their expectations are set far higher and thus will, unfortunately, have further to fall if a depression does set in.

For us in our sixties and older, the 'me' and 'my space', 'my lifestyle' ideas are new. Younger people are adjusting to these modern concepts and it is sometimes difficult to be able to help them. Our experiences have been quite different. Often, it seems, the compromise is one of more equal sharing of responsibilities. But even if the couple don't stay together under the same roof, they can still contribute and help the other with problems.

Is 'I love you' no longer enough for people? Perhaps 'I love you but I want to do my own thing' might be more appropriate. No doubt an acceptable pattern of mutual satisfaction will gradually emerge – it usually does. After all, times change and we adapt.

But in 2009 it is going to take more than a diamond ring to keep a loved one tied to your heart. Have no fear, though, because lovers are optimists and true love will always find a way. Happy Valentine's Day.

12 Snow White

I have always been completely enchanted by Christmas. Mainly for this reason we got married on 30th December on the Saturday between Christmas and New Year in 1961. It was a cold, though sunny day. I was 19 and Tony 24, pretty average ages for getting married in those days. We met on St Valentine's Day, 14th February 1960, at St George's Hall and were married at the Roman Catholic Church of Our Lady Star of the Sea, by Canon Phillips at twelve o'clock. Then we had a sit down luncheon reception at the Hermitage Hotel, now razed to the ground. Mrs Taylor (her husband was my parents' paper-man) was a skilled dressmaker. She carefully made my gown in the front room of her house in the Braye Road, Vale.

Months before I had gone up by train to London from Luton, where we lived at the time, to buy all the material from John Lewis: white Duchesse satin and stiff lining for the full skirted dress with delicate Italian lace for the top and sleeves. My friend Maureen, a Luton girl born and bred, and I had gone up to London for the day to choose the silk, white rose headdress and bouffant net veil, also from John Lewis. Then the whole ensemble had to be transported to Guernsey by me, alone on the mailboat. It was a pretty rough, winter crossing as I recall with the bride-to-be a bit pale around the gills as she disembarked.

A week before our wedding Tony came over from England by plane, waving our licence as he walked down the steps. He looked a bit like Neville Chamberlain declaring peace. But I had had to return to Guernsey for a good few weeks ahead in order to qualify as a Guernsey resident before our marriage.

I dressed for the ceremony at Solidor, our family home. In my great-aunt Lil's bedroom, I had the radio on and clearly remember the song *Steppin' Out With My Baby* as the hit song then. The words were so right for us…'steppin' out with my baby, can't be bad to feel so good'.

Tony chose a charcoal grey suit, white Van Heusen shirt and silver tie. The bridesmaids wore pale blue velvet and blue rosebud headpieces. We didn't have any wedding pictures taken in colour and we both remember being very nervous as our smiles became steadily more fixed.

How excited my mother and mother in law had been, fretting over name places, flowers (pink and white carnations with feathery green fern) and wine. My mother-in-law insisted on going back to the Hermitage twice to rearrange her place settings. Since she didn't drive it was all a bit of a to do as she was ferried back and forth. At last she was satisfied and I don't recall anyone throwing daggers at each other. Mind you, I don't recall very much because I just hated being in the spotlight in those days, especially during the speeches. Tony thanked my father for his 'beautiful daughter' and Laurie Ozanne called out "Hear! Hear!"

My cheeks became very rosy and everyone thought it was the sherry, but I knew otherwise. I just wanted to be alone with my handsome new husband. How strange: I was now Mrs Ozanne, of the Forest Ozanne family, so was no longer the girl Bréhaut from the Vale.

As with the church, The Hermitage hotel was decorated for Christmas looking magical with tinsel lanterns and sparkling lights. We had soup, roast chicken and trifle for a hundred guests. We both came from large Guernsey families – the Bréhauts from the northern parish of the Vale and the Ozannes from the southern, Forest. In fact, we discovered later that we shared the same wedding date with Laurie and Joan Ozanne.

It was all over by four o'clock but several guests stayed on to continue the merriment as a precursor to the next day which was New Year's Eve. We left for the airport and a week's honeymoon in our rented flat in Luton. There was no direct flight to the mainland so we had to fly via Jersey in separate seats. Then it was a train journey to Luton, looking quite exotic, for once, under a snowy white blanket.

The week's honeymoon in our little flat, with a view over frosted rooftops and the muffled quiet that a heavy snowfall brings, couldn't have been more romantic. We lit a small coal fire every morning and the photographs arrived from Guernsey (no videos then) just a week later. A wonderful record of the day we have never forgotten.

Our flat was close to the centre of town. When we ventured out we clung to each other on icy pavements to avoid gritty snow piled up in hardened mounds. But I loved it, having seldom seen 'real snow' like this. There was no traffic, just passers by wrapped up warmly in coats and scarves saying cheery "How do's". Tony bought me a pair of fur lined black boots. They later became very handy for our motor bike rides at weekends. Having purchased bread, milk and eggs we managed to struggle back to our cosy little nest feeling most intrepid.

By the time you read this, our 47th anniversary will be just a few days away. In March, 2009 we are going to see Tony's friend Pete, our best man and Claire, one of our bridesmaids, both from Luton. They themselves married the year after us. Then they left the UK for sunny California, USA. We have all had children, now grown up, who have married and had youngsters of their own. Yet, our weddings seem like only yesterday.

To any couples marrying this month we offer our very best wishes and good luck on your journey together. Winter marriages do seem to last, you know. I wish a happy Christmas to everyone and happy anniversary to Tony.

Are we here now?

Our wedding day, December 1961

13　The Forest Clan

All around me, in St Pierre du Bois, birds (greenfinches, blue tits and wood pigeons) are nesting. Catherine (from opposite) has just given us four goose eggs. The sun is shining and it is spring. It is Easter. It seems only weeks ago that it was Christmas. The cold snap is forgotten and the children have broken up from school.

The sycamore buds are pink with fecundity – leaves barely constrained inside fat, green pods. In the High Parishes (Forest, St Pierre du Bois, Torteval, St Saviour's and St Martin's) there are trees budding everywhere. They are taller and there are more of them than in the Vale and St Sampson's.

A few years after we married we moved to the Forest. This was Ozanne country and I discovered that I had joined a family of remarkably socially active people. Whereas my own relations were, in the main, growers, builders – and before that boatbuilders and stonemasons – the Ozannes numbered a couple of Conseillers, a Jurat, some Deputies and Constables of the parish, teachers and successful businessmen.

They had representatives in the Arts, committees like the Round Table and Rotary, the Forest Church and – most well known – the Hotel industry. Conseiller Bert Ozanne (and later his son Richard) headed the Tourist Board seeing Guernsey through many rich and golden years of success. Richard's brother Martin is now our Education Minister.

The family hotels were White Gables and L'Erée (a popular meeting place for all the Ozanne clan). At White Gables, Elizabeth Ozanne named the new swimming pool *Le Malard* after the field it was built on – drake's pond – and it became a fashionable local venue for members. Now, of course, the Hotel itself is called The Mallard.

My in-laws' house was built in Rue Perrot but was never named – nor did it have a number. Thus, these Ozannes gloried in the address: 'Rue Perrot, Forest, Guernsey' (and every letter got delivered). That house has now been demolished and a new bungalow replaces it. But 'Avondale' and 'Eastleigh', both Ozanne family homes, still exist.

My own ancestral home, 'Solidor', in the Vale still stands (if changed) from my childhood. Our Heaume families also built homes at La Houge and La Grève. The Vale Church cemetery holds most of our ancestors: Heaume, Domaille and Bréhaut. Some of the land was sold to the church by a Domaille, a Jurat. And so was the land (by my Great Aunt Elise Domaille Heaume) where the Vale Rectory is now built.

Left to right: Claude, Bob, Bert, Terry, Len

My Great Uncle and Aunt held the *rentes* to a row of cottages where the feudal court-house of Le Fief St Michel stood. Of this building, the gable end to the road still stands. It is the only part of the original priory (established by Benedictine monks) extant. As a little girl, I remember going with Aunt Elise to collect the money (a peppercorn rent) from the cottage tenants.

I loved the view from Great Aunt Elise's land: on sloping ground overlooking the meadows and Vale Pond. Her greenhouses are gone now and so are the cottages.

In those days, we all 'claimed' our family beaches: L'Islet, Les Ammareurs, Chouet, Ladies Bay, L'Ancresse and Pembroke for us. Fermain, Petit Bôt, Saints Bay, Portelet, Rocquaine and L'Erée for the

High Parishioners.

I still think of Petit Bôt (and Moulin Huet) as somehow a bit out of my league. Getting to Petit Bôt takes a little effort then once on it you have to negotiate all the pebbles. The sun hides behind cliffs quite early on. So a picnic on Petit Bôt needs good timing. Once you are there, though, it is lovely, with the dark greenery and pine trees at the top of the cliff: the wide sandy sweep stretching to clear blue, clean, sea.

When we were courting, we hired Whoopee Floats to paddle across the bay and get a fine tan. Altogether, Petit Bôt was, to me, quite a special and exotic beach, with a uniqueness that it remains to this day.

My first impression, though, of the Forest was the lanes and hedges full of wildflowers. I counted masses of shiny yellow celandines, paler yellow primroses, wild garlic, violets, pink and white campions.

And, in the autumn, my mother-in-law took me to the south cliffs off Le Bigard and Le Corbière. Here we collected purple sloes, growing in hundreds, from her secret spot. Then she made sloe gin, ready for Christmas.

But, for us, the north had the best privately known fishing places. My father kept his crabpots way off Chouet and ormering tides found him in rocks far from the most northern tip of the island.

Last week I asked a fishmonger for some Lady crabs (sometimes called Velvet crabs). But he admitted he hadn't had any for more than four years. Oh, for the Fish Market where, every Saturday in season, you could buy a dozen Lady crabs for your supper. The meat is sweeter and quite unlike the Chancre or the Spider crab. Maybe I will still find some in Brittany or Normandy? They are a delicacy, to be eaten with bread, butter and vinegar, too good to miss. Especially the hard orange roe – the best bit of all.

Another early discovery was that Joan and Lawrie (later Jurat) Ozanne shared our wedding anniversary – December 30th. And Joan and I share a love of the arts. Joan was recently nominated for the Lifetime Achievement Award for all the years of hard work and dedication she has put into the arts for the benefit of the community and her assistance to Edward Chaney in promoting *The Book of Ebenezer Le Page*. Joan has also played an enormous role in getting the Guernsey Lily International Amateur Film and Video Festival off the ground into the hugely successful event it is today – attracting entries from all around the world of the highest standard.

So, this month, we wish thanks and a happy eightieth birthday, to you Joan. And, as we enter the months of re-birth and hope, a Happy Easter, to everyone.

14   The Wireless

Explicit comedians like Jimmy Carr and Russell Brand leave me cold. Give me the wry humour of old boys like Kenneth Horne any day. Comedians and writers on BBC Radio in their heyday were the masters of *double entendre* and innuendo. They were wittier, cleverer and just, well, funnier. Kenneth Williams with his hilarious voice range hammed his scripts up outrageously. The suave Hugh Paddick played the perfect 'straight' foil inviting us listeners to be in the know. We even learnt what some gay slang words meant. Great fun.

Over Sunday lunch, in our little house down L'Islet way, or on the beach with our transistor (all the rage then), we always listened to *Round The Horne* and *The Navy Lark*. We'd laugh out loud and still remember some catch phrases even now. Betty Marsden, as the character Bea Clissold, an ageing Celia Johnson type actress, would be asked something like, "And did you give pleasure to others in The Little Hut [an imagined theatre]?" would reply huskily, "Many times. Many, many times!"

We loved plain silliness like: "What are we having for dinner?" Reply: "Rhinoceros, with rather a lot of chips!"

Today, gratuitous swearing has become so accepted we barely notice it. Reality shows like *Big Brother* and *I'm a Celebrity, Get Me Out of Here* opened the door to language impossible to control since these programmes go out live. Even Jamie Oliver swears, for goodness sake. I prefer his 'pukka' words, calling vegetables names like 'Mr Tomato' and 'these little darlin's'. That is amusing: that makes me smile.

But swearing, really offensive words used to show how 'edgy' (cutting edge) you are, is an abuse of trust for the audience. We know lavatorial humour will always get a snigger but when a whole show consists of this, say in the later series of *Little Britain*, it simply becomes sordid and decidedly unfunny. One answer, of course, is simply to press the off button.

There was something comforting about the signature tunes of *Housewives Choice*, played in the mornings and *The Luscombes* and

The Huggets, sitcoms, on early evenings. Radio had, and still has a more intimate effect on us. It is as though the programme is just for us, whereas on television we are frequently shown the audience – there is even audience participation. So we know that we are but one of very many watching a show. It's not quite theatre, which still does have a one to one feeling if the writing and acting is good and not quite variety show or pantomime.

The comics of variety shows, like Max Wall, Tommy Trinder and Arthur Askey ("I thank yew!") were able to both appeal to the crowd and draw in the lone spectator. Maybe people today would find them lacking? They did rely considerably on catch phrases. The rules have changed. There is now a broader, different set of values, not all of them very high.

Tony with transistor radio, 1960

Going even further back, I remember listening to *ITMA* with my mother when we were in the kitchen together: *It's That Man Again* originally referred to Hitler but later to the great Tommy Handley.

"Can I do you now, sir?" said the character, Mrs Mop. Naughty, yes, but harmless.

Remember Flanagan and Allen and their song *Underneath the arches*? A charming, romantic song. And, Jack Train with his whisky soaked voice who always said "I don't mind if I do?" when offered a drink? *Much Binding in the Marsh* was popular in 1947 with Richard Murdoch and Sam Costa.

I never warmed to *The Goon Show*, although Tony loved it, especially Spike Milligan and his Eccles and Little Jim characters ("He's fallen in the water!") Harry Secombe was Neddy Seagoon and Peter Sellers Major Bloodnock. They all had their own individual punchlines. I preferred *Hancock's Half Hour* with the dour Hancock and his dry, pessimistic outlook on life. One of his stooges was Sid James, another ribald but animated comic. *Carry On* films with Sid James could be a bit near the knuckle, yes, but not unpleasantly so.

I haven't mentioned women comediennes such as Hattie Jacques and Beryl Reid. They had superb timing and didn't rely on shock tactics. Of course, they could be risqué and rely on double meanings but were not deliberately offensive.

The same cannot be said of Jo Brand, who can be highly entertaining but her reliance on women's (and men's) bodily functions bores me. Dawn French, Jennifer Saunders and Victoria Wood are rightly at the very top of their profession. None of these relies solely on vulgar smut. Their acts include fine observations on the human condition. They are all highly watchable so perhaps not easily transferred to radio.

Ray's a Laugh with Ted Ray and Kitty Bluett allowed Ted Ray to show off his ad-libbing skills, learnt from appearing in variety halls. We listened to *Take It From Here* and loved the young married couple, the Glums. June Whitfield and Dick Bentley played Ron – a lazy boy who preferred to be at home cared for by his parents, and Eth who struggled in vain to better herself.

"Ron?" she would say. "Yes Eth?" he would reply. A whimsical little story would follow such as Eth wanting a new sofa. Ron would then worm his way out of the idea and settle back victoriously.

There are some excellent comedians emerging such as Michael McIntyre and Rhod Gilbert. Jack Dee's show *A Lead Balloon* is wonderful. Johnny Vegas makes me laugh but Graham Norton ploughs on one monotonously, seedy track. To hold our attention such entertainers have become increasingly nasty.

One of the funniest, informed and clever communicators at present is Terry Wogan. He will be difficult to replace. Dave Lamb (whose voice we hear on the *Come Dine With Me*) show would be a contender. So, that brings us right back to the power and the glory of the human voice and talented writing, which is what radio is all about. Enough said.

15   A Kind of Living

March 2007

There were far more weddings in my youth. We were always going off to cousins' weddings and receptions. That's where I first tasted sherry: at the Hermitage Hotel. Very dark brown it was, and went straight to my head so that I felt a bit dizzy throughout the speeches. I was 14.

Our own wedding reception was held at the Hermitage Hotel. We had mushroom soup, roast chicken and trifle at a sit down meal with guests' names hand written, on cards. For my mother and mother-in-law, this was the hardest part: whom to sit next to whom? Did they get on with the person opposite as well? But all went to plan.

For my going-away outfit I bought a suit and a white feathery hat from Luton flea market. I am wearing that hat in the picture for another wedding, when my new husband was best man. People said I looked like June Ritchie, an actress who had just starred in a film called *A Kind of Loving* with the actor Alan Bates.

In fact, life in Luton in 1960 was very similar to the life we saw in *A Kind of Loving*. You courted, got engaged and got married. You saved to buy your first home and saved to buy everything that went in it. Few of us had hire purchase. Our parents frowned upon such things. So it took a few years to kit out our first home.

I bought our first plates from Luton's Woolworths. They have all gone now, but I see the same kind on sale on E-Bay, collector's items for about ten times the price I paid. Isn't life strange? And how fashion has changed. The women guests in the picture nearly all wear cotton print dresses – length just below the knee, hats and gloves and carry capacious handbags. White shoes were fashionable, much to my father's disgust. He reckoned white shoes (and pink) were very common.

In those days, the kitchen terrified me. The rules were so strict: 'roll out your pastry on a cold surface – preferably marble'. Marble? Where did you buy marble anything? 'You must clean your oven on Sunday, just after your roast dinner, whilst the oven is still warm.' Well, my first oven didn't belong to us, but to our landlord, Reg. Cleaning this little beast meant trying to eradicate many years of several tenants' cooking.

I soon gave up and we used to go for motor-bike rides instead to see the rolling countryside of Dunstable Downs and Whipsnade Zoo. Still, I persevered with cooking and now enjoy it, having learnt not to be scared to use ready-made pastry (shortcrust, puff and filo – what luxury), nor worry about buying shop-made cakes and tarts. Our grandparents would not hear of such things.

And now I know what a *canapé* means – couch; *en croute* – with a crust; *poire en chemise* – pear wrapped in pastry, like it has a shirt on, and so on. In my early marriage, these cookery terms spelled mystery and were way out of my league. But I have discovered how to freeze food, to make my own stock and soups. It is all rather fun and much more interesting than just buying ready-made dinners.

Yvonne at a wedding in Luton, 1962

My friend Kate was the first of us to serve up dishes like *chilli con carne*, Hungarian goulash and one-pot suppers. But then, that was Kate, always ahead of the game. Another friend swore by cheese fondue parties – quite the in thing in those days, as were Tupperware parties and 'Club Books' when you could buy things for a weekly down payment. Some friends made a little extra cash like that, running 'Club Books'.

Few women worked full time. When you applied for a mortgage at the High Street Banks, any income women earned would not be taken into account. The contraceptive pill had only just come on the market – the banks' reckoned women were too much of a risk, easily falling pregnant and having to leave the workplace.

In *A Kind of Loving* the June Ritchie character gets pregnant and Alan Bates *has* to marry her. His sister, in the film, has the sort of marriage expected by society in the early 1960s: she is the housewife, the husband the breadwinner; they are buying their first house and only then do they 'try for a baby'. It was very difficult to be outside that cultural pattern in our youth. Today's society is as different as it could be from that time.

There was no such thing as 'me time' for women and I only knew two women who could drive and, not only that, had their own car. A two car family – well, that was a really groundbreaking idea. And nurseries for young children had only just begun to sprout up. Even so, it was still quite frowned upon to leave your child in a nursery and a) go to work, or b) do something else but look after the baby, full time.

Yet, mostly, our marriages survived. Of course there were separations and, eventually, divorces occurred. Divorcees were often treated with a kind of suspicion and judged unreliable. The *Guernsey Press* printed a list of divorce cases in the newspaper in those days, naming any co-respondents cited for adultery.

The couple whose wedding is pictured (oh dear, nearly fifty years ago now) actually did separate and divorce after having three sons. Happily, after some years, they re-married each other and are grandparents. They are well and we are still in touch. I don't quite know what that proves, but I wouldn't go back to the early 1960s. Sometimes, it seems, young people have too much, too young and have such freedom it appears positively daunting. Yet, for women in particular, the tide has swung round so that they can make choices of their own and, yes, can be responsible even if they get it wrong. I wish them all good fortune.

16 To Be A Guern

July 2007

Who qualifies as a Guern? Lately we have been asking ourselves this. Well, quite a few people do, it seems. For one thing, there is a French Commune (municipality) de Guern which includes Guern and Quelven, in the region of Brittany, department of Morbihan and is north-west of the district, Le Pays de Pontivy. And very nice indeed the places all look. These 'Guerns' are commonly known as 'Guernattes' apparently. Well, you can't have everything, can you?

Of course, when we Guernsey people talk of 'Guerns' we mean native born and bred Guernsey men and women. The people whose parents and grandparents spoke fluent Guernsey patois as a first language. With their inherited culture came the Guernsey dishes: bean jar, Guernsey gâche and things like brawn made from pig's brains. Real Guerns attended all the horticultural shows, claimed their own 'reserved' places on their 'own' beaches and thought 'their' parish was the best, by far.

True Guerns are proud, almost to a fault, and they would not be anyone else on earth. A stubborn stock, they don't wear their hearts on their sleeves and their tongues are often firmly in their cheeks. So watch out for what they say to you – Guernsey people are their own masters and have merely humouring others down to a fine art. They bow to nobody and are fiercely protective of their family and land.

And a 'Guernsey' can mean our own breed of cattle or a thick knitted jerseyman – sorry, thick, knitted jersey. The Guernsey lily, *Nerine Sarniensis*, an amaryllis, is a large, red lily-like flower and quite beautiful. Not to be confused with the Jersey Lily who wasn't a flower, or a knitted jumper, but Lillie Langtry, born Emilie le Breton, a lady who was very beautiful.

'Guern' should rhyme with 'gurn' (the funny faces pulled by people like Les Dawson) and is not pronounced like the flat, posh version I hear on local television: 'Garnzee' and also 'Jarzee' for Jersey. We Guerns like a good guttural sounding gurn – it is our right.

Permit me a pet hate here when I complain about local television announcers talking like this, "Today in the States…" Excuse me, but could you please add to which island you are talking about? It should be "Today in the States of Jersey…" (which it invariably is) or, importantly, "Today in the States of Guernsey…" or "Today in the States of Alderney…"

While I am at it, could Parishes be clearly identified: Saint Peters in Jersey or St Peters in Guernsey? And Guernsey has a Saint Martin and St Saviour as well as Jersey. We Guerns like to be recognized, thank you. Us "other" islands might be smaller but we pack a punch, you know.

That's made me think of 'milk o punch', a thoroughly Channel Island feast, if ever there was. For the feast of Beltane (Brilliant Fires) great vats of milk, eggs and rum were consumed in prodigious amounts, particularly in Alderney on the first Sunday of May. It meant summer was on its way and that nature, the life force of the world, had begun her work again with healthy livestock, game and plants for food.

Young men would meet not long after dawn and visit each country parish, popping into every pub *en route*. Many years before that they would raid gardens – carrying out the gathering of greenery and spring growth in honour of what was a celebration of the end of winter, the birth of new crops and a pagan god of fertility.

My late father-in-law used to visit Alderney especially for Milk-o-punch Day and I used to think how delicious the drink sounded. It originated from the feast that included mead and oats. Trust us to include rum once mead had stopped being produced in large quantity.

Incidentally, I don't suppose we could re-introduce this ancient spring rite back for, say, a Liberation Day? It would be a bit of fun Deputy O'Hara? No, I didn't really think so.

It is thought that Rocque Balan on L'Ancresse Common could be connected to the 'Beltane' god. Although another school of thought is that there was a Balan family living there once. But I do recall my older uncles and aunts telling us not to play near Rocque Balan: that it had mysterious, unlucky qualities. So we never did and we always respected the ancient menhirs and tombs on the common as well.

We were told not to play in the German-built bunkers, either and one unfortunate child was killed when he suffocated in the bunker in Ruette des Haizes. I needed no discouragement since I disliked being in bunkers and to this day cannot visit the Underground Hospital because of some unseen, hostile force which makes me unable to enter. Maybe it's because I am not a one hundred per cent Guern? Or, probably, more likely, it is because of my over-active imagination?

The patois name for Guernsey is *Guernesi* and a Guernsey man is a *Guernesiais* (with an 'e' on the end for a Guernseywoman). The reason why I am not a true Guern, my grandmother Bréhaut always insisted, is because I was born in Cheltenham, Gloucestershire, England. In 1940 my parents left Guernsey for the safety of the Cotswolds. And my mother is Irish, though also born in England. But my father was a true Guernseyman and my three sisters and my brother were all born in Guernsey so they count as born and bred.

Joey, the Ozannes' donkey, 1917

The fact that there had been a war, that my parents were evacuated and that I had no choice where I was to be born (indeed when – in the middle of a World War) didn't come into it. I wasn't born in Guernsey. Because of this completely arbitrary fact, my children can buy a house and earn a living in Europe if they want to (one parent was born in England). Go figure, as the Americans say.

Guernissement means 'notice to quit' so I'll take the hint and do just that. Have a lovely summer.

17 Summer Days

April 2008

Invited to give a talk to them, I found the wives of Cobo to be all very merry and bright. The group has been together since their members' children were small and since they were young women. I envied them. I have never been a very clubbable person myself.

No, I have always felt to be on the periphery, observing rather than taking part. But you do miss a lot – not belonging to a group of like minded folk. As they listened to me (about writing and publishing) I listened to them.

The point was, they said, to have a couple of evenings a month where they could do something together – without husbands or children getting in the way. They reminded me of my late mother-in-law who gained so much from the Women's Institute. She was clubbable and enjoyed all that the WI and her church groups stood for.

There is camaraderie amongst Guernsey women: islanders who make the most of what our island has to offer. In the photograph, taken at Pleinmont, July 1923, can be seen a Choir picnic. The young women epitomise people of the twenties, relaxing in our lovely island: swimming on a balmy day with their friends. For young people, summer is always endless and carefree.

As they grow older, even now, you will find Guernsey women's work in the summer horticultural shows, in the Eisteddfod and any charitable event you could mention. We have many female friends who offer unpaid help with the blind, the aged, ex-servicemen's widows and Church Fellowships. My mother has a lively, interesting time with her St Paul's Fellowship Group. I much admire them all as, over a nice lunch, they look positively to the future. Still, they are not afraid of discussing traditional beliefs of the past and how they might be relevant today.

At the Cobo Wives gathering we got to talking about special family spots on the beach. Cobo, of course, was for them the best beach in Guernsey. Although some agreed L'Ancresse and Petit Bot have a lot going for them, too. As I have often found, people not born here can often be the staunchest defenders of our island way of life. Yet, shamefully, even after decades of living in Guernsey, they are not always regarded as true 'Guerns'.

Isn't it time we stopped all that kind of snobbery and recognized the contribution of women who have understood Guernsey's worth? Even if, largely, some have followed husbands whose careers meant living in Guernsey, they have, wholeheartedly, made their homes here and participated fully (sometimes far more than born Guernsey women) to the absolute essence of our island.

Summer days, 1923

Of course, there are and always have been, talented business women who, in their own right, take their place in Guernsey society. We can count, thankfully, a growing number of women in law and throughout the finance sector in such highly regarded positions as directors, managers and administrators, in medicine, the church and the teaching professions. There are some special women (I wish I could mention them, but you probably know who they are) who hold key jobs – they are vocational, and work hard for such things as the arts and for sport. Some women work not from offices but from their own homes.

I know that a lot of unsung work is done for children with special needs and some who chair charities for those with disabilities of all kinds. All of them contribute to the society we hold dear. Not all of them were born in Guernsey but, I would wager, would fight to the wire to keep our standards as high as they are against any society you would care to mention.

Time and again we hear of how people are drawn to Guernsey, not only for her heart-stopping beauty but because we have not lost our strong identity. Because we are all in the same small boat in the middle of the English Channel, a stone's throw from the foreign land of France, we have to pull together. We will not tolerate mindless petty crime, graffiti, litter or bullying neighbours. We will not because we cannot.

For the first time in my life I spent Easter in London. Well, Good Friday and Easter Sunday might as well have been any day at any time of year for all the recognition there was of a Christian festival. Yes, there were plenty of chocolate eggs and, on Oxford Street, lots of toy bunnies and endless "Easter" things to buy. But fasting? Spiritual renewal? Jesus suffering? Not one hint of these traditional Easter meanings were evident. I thought that it was extremely sad and gladly returned home.

Later I read in a national newspaper items that were deemed absurd and petty. They were sniggered at and ridiculed at as 'news'. One item was: 'In Jersey a couple were nearly run over.' But, to us in the Channel Islands, this is news. Our news. In national newspapers burglaries and mindless crime are sometimes not even considered for inclusion any more. Well, there is the difference between us: zero tolerance for islanders has to be the norm. For a close community we have to look out for each other, and we do.

In April 'Floral Guernsey' is holding several events. How civilized it will be, to wander around gardens, cliff paths and green lanes. Amongst other things, we will be able to see flowery hedgerows and natural valley gardens, the splendid Guernsey clematis nursery. We can even produce paintings of flowers, if we want to, in Torteval Church Hall.

Taking part in a rather more serious part of our island life will be those women who have bravely stood as candidates in each parish for election to the States of Guernsey. They follow the redoubtable footsteps of women like Blanche Dorey and Norah Wheadon who stood resolutely firm for our Guernsey way of life. We wish them all well. For, after all, their success is also ours.

18 Isabella

June 2007

I have always been partial to a nice hat. A young man in a straw boater, or morning dress top hat, can look most stylish. Think of Ladies Day at Ascot: everyone looks very elegant and glamorous. If not quite in the 'My Fair Lady' league, I myself wouldn't say no to a frivolous creation to wear at the Races. And I do love a wedding with the chance to dress up in something more than everyday clothes.

Sadly, most of today's advertising includes models, men as well as women, wearing hardly anything at all, never mind a hat. It is such a shame. Human mystique is the most potent of weapons in our armoury of attraction to each other. In the 'olden days' a nicely turned ankle was enough to send an admiring gentleman into the vapours. How much nicer than the soft to hard pornography we are regularly dosed with today in newspapers, magazines, films and television.

Marketing of all goods these days includes pushing the frontiers of decency further and further toward just plain vulgarity and the slightly obscene. Models are persuaded to strike poses and wear clothes that leave absolutely nothing to the imagination and you have to be seventeen and shaped like an ironing board to wear most of the clothes. It is debasing and demeaning to the viewer, not just the model.

And it isn't only about clothes, dear me no. It is about anything at all that requires marketing: selling, i.e. making money for the manufacturers. Yes, our old friend: profit. What a shame it all is. Things have to be 'sexed up' – what an ugly expression. It is a lazy term used by copywriters as mindlessly as food manufacturers' ladle salt and sugar into food to tantalise the mass taste buds.

Ladies Bay was called that because that was where ladies bathed. My Great Aunt Elise told me of how, as a young girl, she and all her friends and cousins would go down to the beach in groups and bathe in one of their old cotton dresses (hem down to the ankle). Bathing costumes, as such, had not yet been invented. They would walk into the sea and have a gentle dip, immersing themselves in the water, before drying off and changing back into day clothes.

The men and boys were supposed to bathe at Les Ammareurs, but of course, boys being boys, they had their favourite rocks to hide behind for a bit of spying on the girls. They all had a bit of fun, then, without fear of being harmed.

The Havelet swimming pools in St Peter Port were called 'bathing places' in the old days and also had the women's and men's pools kept separate. As school children we had to have swimming lessons, segregated, in the, often, freezing cold seawater. We used to call out to the boys in their 'men's' pool: singing songs out loud and blushing if and when we got a reply.

Now, I belong to a swimming club and nobody blushes as they strip off naked in the changing rooms – although there may be vacant booths where one could change discretely. Just one more little slice of modesty is cut away to reveal the cheap, common herd in us, rather than our unique individuality that, surely, should be guarded and treasured?

As for sheer beauty and individuality, we are indebted to Mrs Ruth Berry for giving us the delightful photograph of Isabella Carré, taken in Spring, 1900. Mrs Berry, a cousin of my husband, told us that when Isabella (known as Bella) was young she would go into her Aunts' shop – a big shop below the Post Office in Smith Street, where Lovells used to be and which is now Marks and Spencer.

The Aunts were Mantle Makers (cloaks and coats) and Milliners. They used to give Bella one of their new hat creations and she would wear it to go to Town. When people commented upon her fine hat, Bella would tell them they could buy one the same at the Misses Symons shop.

Mrs Berry informs us that opposite the Symons' Smith Street shop was another relative's business: Great Uncle William's. He had a leather shoe shop and they used to make shoes and boots for one of the Queens of England. Mrs Berry's father, in his shop in Trinity Square, had the boot lasts on a shelf for years, but the wooden lasts were stolen during the Occupation, possibly for firewood.

Mrs Berry still has a pair of boots that were made for my husband's Aunt Isabella when she was a young girl, living in the family house near Victor Hugo's in Hauteville. A handed down story is that one of the Carré family was a friend of Hugo's and regularly played chess, or bridge, with him. My husband's grandfather James Carré, Isabella's future husband, was known as 'Pop Carré' and he had a chemist shop in the Bordage.

While writing, well done to Mrs Berry for still driving her car competently in her late nineties and for writing a letter with such clear, fine handwriting. She reminds me of some of the Guernsey women I knew as a girl: independent and strong.

Isabella, 1900

I recall my female relations – women who were modest, thrifty and house proud and, like the men of Guernsey, loyal to each other and their island. But try making them do something that they would prefer not to and you would find the stubbornness we are famed for. And you were not let into their close circle easily. You had to earn their friendship. The other side of a close community was that you had to mind your own business, or people would do it for you: keeping of secrets, retaining your own counsel, is an islander's special art.

And as for the photograph of Isabella? What a wholly benign era that was – when advertising of your goods merely meant the wearing of a pretty hat to Town, to help out your Aunts.

19 Budloe, Nipper and Titch

September 2008

There I was, ever so pleased to be a *hann'taon*, a cockchafer – the nickname for a Vale-ite because it went so well with the Cock of the North and my favourite creature is a cockerel. The proud cockerel at the tip of the Vale Church has always been one of my favourite symbols. But my rude awakening was learning that a cockchafer is actually a brown beetle.

Now that we live in St Peter Port we fare no better since we are now *cllichards* – spitters – and that doesn't leave much to the imagination. How much better to be a Forest-ite, like my husband is, and be a *bourdon* – a bumblebee. If we still lived in St Pierre du Bois we would be *etcherbaots* – beetles again. So perhaps I am a natural beetle rather than anything to do with poultry, symbolic or otherwise.

St Sampson's folk are *roines* – frogs, Castel *anes-pur-sang* – pure blooded donkeys, St Saviour's are *fouormillaons* – ants, St Martins's *cravants* – ray fish, St Andrew's *les croinchaons* – the siftings – because of all those quarries, I expect and poor old Torteval are – donkeys with horses' hooves, which seems vaguely satanic.

A true Guernseyman is often known by his nickname. My father's friends had a splendid crop between them: Big Wick, Little Wick, Ferpo, Beaver and Titch. His own was Winno instead of Edwin. So it was lovely to read a recent obituary of what was a relatively young man (anyone who is not over seventy is young to us now). Not only did his funeral service take place on the grassy bank outside his favourite pub, with superb views over Rousse, toward Chouet, but his friends' names were a delight. Somehow, men called Curly, Yogi, Chico, Nipper, Podge and, my favourite, Budloe, cannot be anything but born and bred Guerns. (A *budloe* is an effigy much like Guy Fawkes, burnt on bonfire night. In fact the word is derived from the Guernsey French *patois* for yule log) Anyway, good for all of you and good for the late Guernseyman, too.

Even in such a small island, particular areas have a different feel to them. To me, the Vale will always mean wandering over the common, bordered with pungent yellow gorse, prickly with furze and fern. The long stretches of sand of Ladies Bay, Pembroke and L'Ancresse are best walked in winter, with a cold wind blowing behind you. A transparent sheen, left by a receding tide makes a mirror for the sky. I have just bought a painting by Jennifer Collas who has captured, exactly, this entrancing corner of the island with her picture of Pembroke. She has included the liquorice brown vraic with its long tails that we used to collect and have battles with as children. We used to swipe each other quite hard. Oops, hope the health and safety police aren't reading this. If you note a Jennifer Collas exhibition advertised again be sure to go and see it. You will be delighted.

At Steam Mill Lane: the Carré children with their donkey and trap

As for St Andrew's, I do hope they are allowed to keep their school. It is so obviously important for their community. You will know by now what the outcome was and whether the parents, teachers and children have lost or won their battle. How long will we see all concerned walking determinedly to school with their specially made yellow jackets? Are their days numbered and St Sampson's infants equally fought for, or will their determination have paid off? I shall be interested to see what has happened and if anyone listened to their heartfelt plea.

St Andrew's and Castel have some of our best, breathtakingly beautiful, unspoilt countryside. The parishes boast whole swathes of rolling green fields, valleys and hedgerows, thick with wildflowers and woody plants. Yes, the southern parishes have their glorious cliff walks but have always seemed – it's a childhood prejudice I daresay – rather grand to me in both senses of the word. Moulin Huet, Petit Bôt and Fermain Bay, with their triangle of blue sea at the bottom of steep hills either side, were a day trip out in my younger days. I have the same feeling in Sark: it is almost too fabulous, bordering on an overwhelming beauty.

For now, I miss waking up in St Pierre du Bois, to our neighbour Catherine's plump white geese calling in the morning air in their enchanting little meadow. Nearby you could hear a cockerel crow and it was always a pleasure to wake to such natural sounds. On some stormy nights you could hear the sea crashing and echoing into the rocks and gulleys of Havre des Bon Repôs.

Because there are no fields or tractors for the seagulls to pick up delicious morsels, there aren't so many here near Mount Hermon. Of course, once you get nearer the harbour there are great flocks of them, following the boats and scrabbling noisily over leftover food. But I do miss the everyday, morning sound of seagulls. They used to wheel and circle over our roof, even eyeing bread left out for garden birds. I am glad when the seabirds venture out our way. To compensate, one can see the most glorious dawns from the east in town, from the first rising light to melting yellow, green, pale blue and lavender sky. Lovely.

St Sampson's always meant greenhouses, the Saltpans, fishing and the busy, working harbour of The Bridge. The South Side, of course, was our unspoken boundary. We would to play on Delancey Park but it never seemed quite like ours, not like the common. Quite swiftly the parish slips into St Peter Port parish, with its air of sophistication, full of people we didn't know.

Yet still the seagulls wing the sky all over our island, uniting us Guernsey donkeys as we enter a different season. The sun is lowering and today sees the Autumn Equinox. Soon we will be gathering sloes for sloe gin; the blackberries have been going for a long time and there are ripening red apples and golden pears simply everywhere. Another summer is gone but we can soon enjoy those windy walks with a crackling good fire to sit by when we get home, if we are lucky, and Guernsey people certainly are.

20 Sark

November 2004

We have all visited Sark, 'that rare blend of simplicity and sophistication', says the Tourist Guide, 2004. So, in a recent television programme, when an Australian family did an exchange with an English one (who visit Sark once a year) but the Aussies hated it, had us enraged.

How could people come to the island, where we have always enjoyed leafy lanes and the superb La Seigneurie Gardens – possibly the best of its kind in Great Britain; an atmosphere of magical mystery complete with freshly caught fish and cream teas – complain?

How dare they! Yet, dissenters are within their rights. We, in Guernsey, also live in a special place. But we are on dangerous grounds if we do not allow 'outsiders' to say what they think is wrong. Or, even, what is right. My mother, of Irish descent, knows much more of our family's history than my father, a true and loyal Guernseyman, knew. Yet she loves Guernsey, recognizing it as a 'spiritual' place. She is 85 on November 25th, 2004, and still feels the same.

Sark is certainly a spiritual place, as well. How exciting it is to draw close to Sark's rugged granite cliffs, as the boat arrives from Guernsey. Excitement mounts as, having managed the sea voyage successfully, we gaze down at the deep green sea, then toward Maseline Harbour. We have arrived! Just the steps up to the harbour to negotiate, with people jostling us for position, then, at last, to the safety of the sunny pier.

A queue for the tractor (which we have fondly nicknamed 'the toast rack') then we chug up the dusty Harbour Hill, waving to the hardy souls who have opted to walk. At the top of the hill, another world awaits. Where else do horses and carts make you feel so happy? Sark begins to cast its spell.

Firstly, a rush to book a cart. The driver is always patient. The children take turns to hold the reins. As the horse clip-clops its familiar way, knowing every turn, every hedge and path, we stare in awe at Sark's sheer beauty.

Cottages hide behind thick-leaved trees, their gardens an impossible

Sark trip 1972

Le Seigneurie

Local catch being raffled

perfection. Scents, of hydrangea, of the sea, of horsey sweat and farmyards, assail our lungs. The smells of Sark are unpolluted by any road fumes. All is pure and astoundingly fresh.

Very soon we become light-headed with such uncontaminated air. Through shaded lanes, dappled with sunlight, we plod slowly, the cart creaking, toward Hotel Petit Champ for lunch. We sit outside in blazing sun, no cloud of car waste to stop the rays warming us. Look! We can see Guernsey! Our little island looks strange from this angle. But how good it is to be off it, and sitting here, for a change.

Eating crab salad, fresh lobster, bread and Sark butter, we feel our tensions uncoil. Sark weaves its magic and for one whole day, we forget our worries. Just as, in Herm, you always catch the sun, in Sark you always feel better.

Where else in the world, either, can you see a sheep race, with jockeys of teddy bears? It is laughable, and we laugh uproariously. That is the charm of Sark: you can be young again. Nobody minds.

We walk across La Coupée. Although the views down to the beach, with its private cove and sparkling sea, are marvellous, I am glad when we go back. La Coupée is just a little too awe-inspiring for me.

La Seigneurie garden never fail to impress. There is a timeless gorgeousness to it. We wander around, getting lost in the maze, silently congratulating the gardeners, whoever they may be.

Then, onto the town, which came to a unique standstill in time many years ago. People, of all shapes and sizes and of all ages, ride rickety bikes. Some have clearly not ridden for some time, wobbling and falling off constantly. The children whizz by with glee, ringing their bicycle bells, delighted to be let off their leashes. No cars!

We buy knick-knacks and baseball caps from the old-fashioned shops, looking like the shanty houses of a cowboy film. By now we are different people from those who landed in Sark a few hours ago.

To the pub, then, to take a break and talk about our trip. In the pub raffle, someone wins a whopping lobster weighing over five pounds. We are very envious.

Soon, we must take the tractor down the hill again. This time we are laden with souvenirs and memories or our day. Next time we'll visit the beaches, or swim in a hotel pool, or go for a long rambling walk.

The Australian family on the television programme said that there wasn't much to do. There certainly isn't, if you want entertainment laid on. Sark doesn't do passive. And the children wanted food like you get at McDonalds. Shame, really, but then the food on Sark is an acquired taste: seafood so fresh it jumps around the plate; butter so rich it is orange coloured; home-made chocolates, sinfully delicious.

Yet, the Australians were entitled to their point of view. Sark isn't perfect. I had friends who stayed there in a self-catering cottage. They had to leave after a few days, so haunted did they feel the island was. They were born Londoners, so maybe the spiritual vibes were too strong for them?

We joined them, one misty day, cycling around the cliff paths. As the grey wisps of haze swirled around us, John, the Londoner, said, "Don't you feel the atmosphere is, well, thick with – witches brew?" I told him we had just been to the pub, perhaps that was it, too much ordinary brew? We laughed, but I did understand.

Back in Guernsey, walking along the White Rock to our cars, I could see Sark in the distance. It is definitely a mysterious place. Ah well, maybe Aussies don't do mysterious.

21   Cloud of Iona

May 2007

As much as the sea, Guernsey people rely on aircraft and clear skies to connect them to the rest of the world. And nowadays flights can be ridiculously inexpensive and take us to un-thought of places that were once the prerogative of only the very rich.

On May 9th, Liberation Day – still, essentially, the Guernsey people's very own day – is when our thoughts go back to our liberation from the Occupation of enemy forces and to the Air Force, Navy and Army services of the 40s. It is our own special day and nowhere else in the world knows exactly what it means to us. It is a silent salute to the men and women who lived through the terrible time of war, separation and uncertainty.

It is a day to wave the Guernsey flag. Liberation Day is a kind of moving forward from spring into summer and all that that can mean to islanders.

My father was an aviation enthusiast and served in the Royal Air Force in India with the Air-Sea Rescue. He would have been interested to learn that Squadron Leader Neville Duke, who died in April of this year and who was decorated six times for gallantry before becoming a renowned test pilot, was still flying his own aircraft at 85. Whilst flying with his wife in his own aircraft, Duke suddenly felt unwell but managed to land safely before collapsing and dying later that same evening. A hero until the very end.

A seaplane, the *Cloud of Iona*, amongst other things took part in the Highland Games in Scotland and was acquired by Jersey Airways – you could say the *Iona* was the Aurigny of its day.

In 1936, my father and his friends decided, as young men in their twenties, to visit Jersey for the day. They attempted to book five seats on the *Cloud of Iona* but could only obtain four. They wanted to travel together, so they booked five seats to Jersey the day before they had originally chosen. Incredibly, the very next day – the day they would have been on board, the *Cloud of Iona* crashed into the sea south of Jersey with all lives lost. Very sadly, eight passengers and two crew – all wearing life-jackets – were found washed up on the French coast a week later.

All the five Guernseymen pictured remained in close friendship for many years. They lived at a time when Guernsey was still truly theirs. They played golf together, sailed boats, fished and knew the stars, the tides, the dangerous currents and the very rocks of the Channel Island seaways. From schooldays, their interests and horizons were the same. The photograph shows five young men relaxing in the sun of 'the other Channel Island' at their ease in the casual clothes of their day and before World War Two when their lives and the all the Channel Islands were about to be changed forever.

Left to right: Wilson Farnham, Beaver Sebire, Billy Creber, Edwin ('Winno') Bréhaut, Johnny Heaume, at Grève de Lecq, Jersey, 1936

How many parties of young men today would be content, now, with a day out in Jersey as a holiday? Even in the 1960s we dressed up in our best for air travel to Jersey, seeing it every bit as foreign as France.

My very earliest memory is of one Sunday promenade that my parents took from home to walk to and all around Les Ammareurs, Pembroke and L'Ancresse. My father and Bert (Beaver) Sebire were not unalike in looks and I recall my father holding me, aged four, as I peeped over his shoulder at Mr Sebire who lived with his wife near Lucksall and Mr Sebire was trying to make me smile. Not having seen my father for four years I confused him with Mr Sebire and couldn't understand what was going on. Who were these two men and why did they look the same? I felt very shy and nervous.

But, even then, I could sense the kind of safe camaraderie they shared. Our whole world centred on my parents' group who all lived no more than two miles away from us. As children we often explored the grassy stretches of L'Ancresse, with its flourishing golden gorse bushes and ancient stone monuments – which I actually thought always smelled damp and were a bit creepy. We would regularly see my father's friends out golfing and we knew them all by name.

Indeed, they left a legacy of friendship that lasted to the end of their lives. I was tempted to write 'we shall not see their like again', but, really, that is not true. There are plenty of Farnhams, Sebires, Crebers, Heaumes and Bréhaut families alive, well and thriving in Guernsey and who still live much as their forefather's did and who hold much the same values and their love of island life. The little piers and harbours, common land and beaches that were our fathers' are still here.

Beautiful Les Mielles still overlooks Les Houmets, Herm, Alderney, Sark and France on a clear day. You can still walk without seeing a car nor hearing an aeroplane in this most northern part of Guernsey. The north is still a wonderful place for ormering. Still, at low tide, you can see what there is left of the *Iris*, wrecked in 1918 off Fort Le Marchant.

And, if it weren't for fateful chance none of us would be here. But Guernsey's rocks will always remain. Whatever happens the same, awesome sea will still surround us and the ever-changing sky will forever canopy above the island. Makes you think, doesn't it?

22   Imagination Counts

September 2006

I have always had a rich imagination: both a blessing and a curse in equal measures. Yes, it's nice to arrive in a country and possess the creative process, recording and writing about where you are and the place you are visiting. But getting there in the first place? Ah, there's the rub.

My first plane trip, 1958, involved my not breathing for about an hour and a half, not talking, keeping my coat on and sitting stiffly in my seat. Well, you had to, I reasoned, otherwise the pilot would get distracted. You mustn't laugh, eat or talk. Because the instant you stop paying absolute attention, concentrating on where the plane was heading then, obviously, it would drop straight out of the sky.

No, I had to shut my eyes (never look out of the window and actually *see* how far up we are. Miles up in the air? How did we get there? How can a big, heavy metal machine be flying above the clouds? That is a ridiculous concept and I do not want any proof.)

What if the pilot has had a row with his wife and is not focusing? Worse – what if he has had a row with his mistress? It didn't bear thinking about.

So, no, having an imagination is not always a good thing. In fact it can be a real nuisance. Dentists – now there is a haven of fertile soil for the creative seeds of the imaginative. I only need one filling. Yes, but what if the dentist has a heart attack just at the very moment the whining drill is aimed at my poor tooth?

What if I choke? What if the dental nurse distracts the dentist by fainting at a critical point?

Worse than all of this is mathematics. I was fine until I reached about nine years old. I went to the Vale School (1950s, don't ask) and my teachers, as I recall, all seemed nice enough, except, perhaps, my maths teacher was a tad strict. She had a severe expression and this is where all the trouble started.

You see, I think I may have discalculia – the numbers version of dyslexia – or maybe 'maths phobia'.

Numbers were so puzzling because '3' (a number) could also mean 'three' (a word) and 'three' and 'three' put together made 'six' (a different number and word) yet '3' and '3' made '6'. Or, again, something could weigh '3lb 3ozs' and still be 'three pounds and three ounces'. And 'pound' weight could also mean 'lb' and ounce 'oz'. Then there was '£', a pound, which was also a paper note. And so on and on.

Yvonne at Solidor aged 14, 1956

Mental arithmetic was a nightmare and I still avoid it if possible. Clocks, calendars, timetables and measuring tapes frightened the life out of me. All those numbers meant something else, like time, months, schedules of journeys and widths of waists. I wish I had a pound (£) for every time I got mixed up!

Getting back to mental arithmetic, it still made very little sense to me. Why on earth – I wanted to ask my teacher, but was far too scared – would two boys go to a camp site farm. One buys three eggs at 4 pence each, the other buys 2 eggs but, because they are brown, he pays 6 pence each. How much did each boy pay for their eggs?

Well, I would ponder. Why would two boys want all those eggs? What on earth were they going to do with them? Did their mothers know? Were they brothers? Who was the oldest? Would he be doing the cooking? What an awful thing if they burnt themselves making an omelette. The

83

Scoutmaster ought to be ashamed of himself.

At this point my stern teacher's face would be an inch from mine as she turned puce, rapping my desk with her stick. Teachers had sticks in those days and jolly well used them, too.

"Yvonne! How much did each boy pay for his eggs?"

Well, I had forgotten by then what the question was, never mind the answer.

What about men mowing lawns the size of cricket pitches – "how many yards has he mowed if he mows at three yards a minute?" you get the drift. I just felt so sorry for the man. Couldn't he have got some help? Did the lawn have hedges? I have always thought cricket pavilions look really romantic…

Yes, a rich imagination has its downside. I was fine with algebra (letters, you see, x, y and z) that made sense. X of something added to Y of something came to Z. Abstract. I can do abstract.

Same with geometry until it got a bit advanced – after all I wasn't about to build a house or design a boat. But I was quite happy with perimeters, circumferences and right angles.

As for decimals and long division, my poor teacher at the Intermediate School for Girls (before it was the mixed gender Grammar School) actually gave up on me entirely.

Only after a patient mathematician explained accounting pictorially, have I got to grips with basic maths. Now, I can perfectly well see that 'A' account is for putting numbers in, 'B' for taking out and 'C' has to balance up the lot. I even managed foreign currency bank accounts with this mathematics expert as my teacher.

I used to want answers to what seemed to me to be quite simple questions. For example: if everyone else knew that '3' and '3' make '6' why was it so darned important for me to know? I only had to ask someone to find out. This was, of course, before pocket calculators were invented, thus solving the whole issue for me.

After all, numbers are not like reading, which is pleasurable and educational, nor painting where you express what you see.

Calculations seemed, somehow, irrelevant. But I perfectly accept that I simply do not possess a 'mathematical' side to my brain. I have, though (just so I don't come over as completely crackers), been told that I am a lateral thinker.

Well, there you are, then – that must count for something, mustn't it?

23 An Opening Door

February 2004

I well remember coming home from school and telling my mother that I hadn't heard my name. It was the 11-plus results and, in those days, 1953, pupils going to one of the Colleges or Grammar Schools ('Boys' and 'Girls', then and called 'The Intermediates') were read out alphabetically. My surname was Bréhaut so I knew pretty soon that I wasn't on the list.

We were surprised because I had always done well and was in the A stream. It was lunchtime. We didn't expect Mr Roy Carré, the Vale School head teacher, to arrive to explain that I was borderline. My maths had let me down badly, as they do to this day.

Mr Carré suggested that my parents consider fee-paying to the Girls' Grammar School (which was a choice available then) as I was, he thought, academically able. The fees were less than those for the Ladies College and so it was that I began my secondary school career in St Peter Port.

Although I always had A-grades for English Language, Literature and Art and enjoyed French, History, Geography and Biology, my maths had always been a problem. The assessment at 11 had been correct. In maths lessons it was a constant, miserable struggle to keep up with the others.

But witnessing the Girls' Grammar School being demolished is very sad. Our teachers in the early fifties had just come through the Second World War. The majority were single women with degrees. You could say they were vocational. I used to love hearing about the holidays they took together: Rome, Rimini, Crete – the places sounded exotic and the historical sites and art they saw marvellous. I vowed to go to those places one day.

We had cookery lessons at Granville House where I made totally inedible pies. And we had sewing lessons where I made an unwearable shirt in yellow Aertex. My mother used it as a duster. The values of the Grammar School included an expectation that you had such things as indoor and outdoor shoes, hockey sticks and a whole range of expensive equipment. You did things called 'prep' (homework) and got conduct marks and detention for bad behaviour. It was quite formal and no-nonsense. I learnt to dread some lessons with certain teachers but to acquire a lasting love of books and the library, music and art.

At fourteen plus we were streamed into GCE O-levels (forerunner of GCSE) or RSA (Royal Society of Arts), i.e. secretarial training. In those days there was no setting, and you had to be good at all subjects to be considered able to study any GCEs in the Sixth Form. It was academic or not. So, very much against my English and Art teachers and indeed my own wishes, I entered the RSA stream, taking English, Shorthand, Typing and Book-keeping.

The careers open to girls then were teaching, nursing and secretarial. Very few went on to University. So, together with personal family reasons, my hopes to read English or attend Art College disappeared and I became a secretary.

But I never lost my appetite for knowledge and the Arts. Eventually married and with two young children, I attended evening classes in English, Art and Sociology for several years. After gaining GCSEs at O- then A-level I wondered if I could, after all, study for a degree.

Eventually I sent off for an Open University prospectus. The courses were so enticing, it was like entering a sweet shop. Once I had gained one credit (you need six to qualify and two of those must be at 3rd or 4th level for an Honours degree) I realised that I could do it.

Alan Bisson was my Foundation (first course) tutor. He was helpful and encouraging to all of us. My first tutorial with Alan was held at Granville House, and the irony was not lost on me! Peter Pannett, also, has always been a fount of information and support. Both Alan and Peter are still very active in the OU, Guernsey.

Over the next seven years I studied an Arts Foundation Course, Modern Art and Modernism, European Culture and Belief 1450-1600, Art in Italy, the Classical Renaissance 1480-1580, Philosophy of the Arts, The Enlightenment, and Managing in Organisations, my only technical course. The courses included history, literature, art, English, music, theology, anthropology, philosophy, architecture and much more.

Studying for me means a minimum of 14 hours a week, written essays which are assessed (called Tutor Marked Assessments) tutorials and examination. I went on five residential courses, called Summer Schools, held at universities in London, Bath, East Anglia and Preston. The States of Guernsey assisted with travel, accommodation and tutorials. When I did them Guernsey was the only place in Britain covering these costs without a means test. Well done the States of Guernsey on that.

Most lecturers at Summer School (and tutors) come from other universities and colleges and most often have full-time jobs already. It was wonderful for me to have a one-to-one lecture by an Oxford Don in front of a Picasso at the Tate. Especially since he had written some of our textbooks. I felt I had, at last, truly experienced university life.

Another occasion I valued was being instructed to go to the National Gallery in London, select a slide (I chose Madame Moitissier, by Ingres) and then give a talk about it. This was my first lecture. We had been studying Ingres. All the other students had to do the same, choosing their own slide and topic, and we spent our last evening at the Summer School each doing our lectures.

Each Summer School has a project to which all students contribute. My last Summer School was for Philosophy of the Arts, a third level course. By now I was a seasoned student and was even able to be of some help to some of the others. That was very rewarding indeed.

I didn't meet one lecturer or tutor who wasn't highly involved and committed to teaching us. The teaching, textbooks and other aspects are of a very high standard. In turn, they told me, they enjoyed teaching motivated students – which most OU students are, by definition.

It can be lonely if you are the only student doing a certain course. Obviously, there can't be local tutors for every course. Guernsey students do suffer a disadvantage there. Students on the mainland can attend not only regular tutorials, but weekend workshops, special tours and exhibitions.

But living here, as we all know, has its drawbacks as well as advantages. We have to make the best of it. I didn't have a computer during my first time with the OU, and I imagine nowadays it is enormously helpful with studies if you have access to OU materials and the Internet. This time around (studying a French foundation course) I already feel the benefits of e-mail, keeping in touch with fellow students and accessing excellent OU information. I have just bought a CD-ROM with which I can record my voice and ask questions.

Is it difficult? Yes, of course it is. At degree level you are expected to have read and understood your textbooks and to contribute far more than at A-level, say. The OU guides you and provides first class texts and does not let you get away with sloppy thinking. (The Quality Assurance for Higher Education had rated 86.7 per cent of the subjects offered by the

OU as excellent. This beats many top universities' scores.)

For your money you get CDs, videos, books, background booklets, online support and full explanations of the courses offered. The OU also have a media department supplying optional CD-ROMs, videos and books at extra cost, but linked to your course.

All I can say is that it has been an engrossing adventure. I am now studying French, this time not to get a degree, but just to understand French and France's culture.

Now in my sixties, my biggest problem is memory. But I have met many students who had disabilities. One man had cerebral palsy and was a wonderful character and happily studying Art History with the aid of a helper. At my graduation ceremony in Brighton, another man, totally blind, went on to the stage complete with white stick to accept a First for his BA Honours degree in English Literature from the Open University Chancellor. His success brought the house down and he had a standing ovation. It was very moving.

I met people who had had truly dead-end jobs and were now qualified, doing research in all fields of endeavour. One woman had been a cleaner and had gone on to have her own department at a London University, teaching tutors. She was a real scholar.

The typical student is somebody wanting to advance but for whom attending university has not been possible. There can be a great many reasons for this. Age is immaterial, indeed students are getting younger as top-up fees loom with other universities. People come from all fields: in education, medicine, clerical positions and law. There are shop assistants, policemen, housewives and retired people but the majority are in full or part time employment.

On the higher level courses you can be studying alongside someone who has a PhD and simply wants to keep up with the latest information. Or it may be a hospital porter who wants to understand Mozart, or a psychiatric nurse with a yen to write a novel. I majored in the Arts, but obviously the OU has maths, science, social sciences and technology modules– the full range of university courses.

I have now lectured on the Italian Renaissance and Impressionist art, have a collection of hundreds of slides, a good library and enjoy travel in Europe. Each London trip includes art galleries, museums and exhibitions. I regularly visit the Institute of Contemporary Arts (the cutting edge institution for new art – see the next Turner Prize winner here) the

British Museum and the Royal Academy of Arts (by the way they have the best coffee shop).

I have visited galleries in cities such as Athens, Paris, Nicosia, Rome and Florence. I am about to go to Venice and next year will visit the Alhambra in Granada, Spain. I did get to Crete and Italy and still remember those teachers, all those years ago, who inspired me to travel in sunny southern Europe and to study ancient history and art.

We have a Labour government to thank for conceiving and getting the Open University off the ground, and I do so, without hesitation. I am naturally of a conservative nature, so do not say this lightly. The Open University offers a first class education to anyone willing to apply themselves.

The University did not want to be *just* a correspondence course. The courses are challenging and the OU degree highly respected. If you have ever thought about studying with the OU, then do it. My only regret is that I did not study and graduate much earlier.

My graduation souvenir programme listed the graduates' names. This time, mine was on it. I had gained a BA Honours Degree. The Open University offers opportunity, opens doors and opens minds.

It has changed my life, forever.

Brighton, 1993

24   For the Love of Art

August 2008

The initiative shown by our new Culture and Leisure minister is a good one. The department want us to tell them what we would like to see developed in the areas of arts and leisure activities. Similarly, the Guernsey Arts Commission has made a cracking good start in 'providing an identifiable voice for the arts in Guernsey, raising public awareness and promoting the value, relevance and social importance of the arts.' Particularly, I was delighted to attend top sculptor, Anthony Gormley's talk at the new Princess Royal Centre and to see his intriguing art set on our very own Castle Cornet. What a coup it was to get Gormley and his important work here. Well done Joanna Littlejohns and Eric Snell.

My own interest in culture began with art. I cannot remember a time that I did not draw and scribble. Writing stories also began at a very young age. I wrote 'cliff-hangers' when I was around eight. I would take the tales down to Les Ammareurs and tell them to my younger cousins, all sitting in a circle on the sand. I have always had a driven nature, wanting to create things and communicate.

The downside, as there always seems to be, was that, whilst I had no trouble in gaining 'A's for the humanities, my attempts at mathematics were tortuous. I left school at sixteen. I have spent the rest of my life gaining the education that I would have liked.

I became interested in both the painting of portraits and of other artists. My first visit to London's National Gallery was when I was seventeen when I marvelled at Rembrandt, Van Gogh and the landscapes of Constable. It was many years before I discovered the Impressionists at the Tate Gallery, the Royal Academy in Piccadilly and the British Museum. An Open University degree with the OU's superb standards literally opened up a vast vista of knowledge. Now these galleries are like friends and we take our granddaughters to see them as a matter of course.

Getting to Athens and the Parthenon, Florence, with its Uffici Gallery and the Bargello – which houses my favourite *David* by Donatello, Rome and Michaelangelo and fabulous Venice with its Titians and Bellinis took a lot longer. But viewing all of this breathtaking art, architecture and sculpture was well worth the wait.

A lifeline for some is their Christian faith, with me it is also 'The Arts' – possibly for the same reasons, for aren't these God given? When you look at Michaelangelo's *Pieta* in the Vatican City, St Peter's Basilica, isn't your heart raised, viewing what mankind is capable of doing? In the midst of base cruelty, terrorism and mindless vandalism there are people who can create beautiful, inspiring art, literature and music.

Man cannot live by bread alone and without the arts we cannot fully live a complete life. We should make the arts not only more intellectually accessible to the young but actually more tangible. By this I mean I would

like to see more talks on art of the quality of Mr Gormley's. He explained that art should not only be found in museums but in everyday places like beaches and open, public places like Castle Cornet. There is going to be an Arts and Islands Conference in September when Mr Gormley will be lecturing again.

All Guernsey students should go to this, not only those taking art as a chosen subject. They should be offered lectures with slides and given visits to the major cities housing art: London, Florence, Rome, Venice, Madrid and Paris to name a few. How excellent it would be if students could discuss the difference between Monet and Manet, Bellini and Bernini as a matter of course. After all, today's youngsters are scatter-gunned with images all the time with things like Facebook on the internet, television, DVDs, videos and cinema. Tell them the importance of knowing what an icon means. What is a Byzantine icon

Donatello's David, *Bargello Museum, Florence*

Self portrait, 1969

and what is its importance to all art? Well, icon means 'image'and from the Byzantine icons artists slowly developed recognisable styles of their own, rather than only producing anonymous, though instantly recognisable, art.

Children are more than capable of interpreting the similarities and differences of Picasso and Braque during their Cubist period. I truly believe that 'Art' isn't 'above' anyone, it simply has not always been taught the way everyone can understand or indeed take an interest in.

During my lectures on the Italian Renaissance students always amazed me at how they quickly they began to comprehend a picture that had previously been indecipherable to them. There is a language of art. Like everything else in life, you know how once you have been taught how.

Some reject 'Graffiti art', seeing it as merely graffiti – vandalising walls – and don't see that kind of art as true art. But Graffiti art has its place in the history of art. It is a cousin of Expressionism, where there are no boundaries to the expressing of an idea. No artistic boundaries that is.

Now, with many more young people going on from Guernsey to attend university, art and technical colleges we have an environment – at last – where art (usually a poor second to sport) is being taken seriously. For with art and culture, we can understand ourselves more. If we understand more about ourselves and about our history we have more chance of making the world a better place for everyone. Without an understanding (or even a fear of) words or concepts like 'beauty' and 'sublime' an entire aspect of life could be lost to our youth. And that would be a tragic loss for all of us.

25 Our Vale Church

January 2008

The Vale Pond and the Vale parish church are inextricable, aren't they? The wildlife reserve is so perfect a setting that we could be forgiven for thinking that the two have always been in existence together. Of course they haven't, the church being first on the scene by a long chalk. The priory came first, around AD962, with the gradual building of the church as we know it taking place over several hundred years.

The pond was formed after the Braye du Valle reclamation, being part of the sea before that. I have always liked Pond House built in the early 19th Century. How wonderful to live overlooking such a beautiful scene, complete with the Vale meadow and little L'Islet bay just over the way.

My picture is painted from the viewpoint of our family home, in Solidor's attic. This lovely view has changed a little – my Aunt Elise sold her greenhouses and the Rectory is now where they used to be. My painting was done around 1968 and we joke that the lady in the foreground is my mother on her way to Lowe's shop at the crossroads of Route Militaire. It won an Honours in the Eisteddfod, with the adjudicator saying it reminded him of a Constable. I thought I would mention that in case you thought all I could do was write (you already know that I can't count). My painting takes a very back seat right now and mild arthritis hasn't helped.

Sorry, I digress. The Vale pond, the church and meadow played a major part in our young lives. This was before the land became part of the National Trust and the McCathie nature reserve not yet founded. You could walk through it then if Mr Quevatre's cows were not munching the luscious green grass, in fact often if they were. Streams flowed into the pond: real streams, not *douits*. Many a tadpole and frog lurked in the muddy banks and I recall many butterflies flitting about in the grasses of the meadow.

My parents used to look out for a lone heron standing with his long legs in the Vale pond. He came each year. And, in talking to Olive Marquis, née Heaume (so we are distant relatives) she told me that she had once seen a preening Kingfisher on the pond. Olive has lifelong links with the Vale church: she used to go with her mother when she was six when her mother cleaned the church. Olive was in the choir, used to ring the bells and was married there. Later she and her husband Bob took care of the altar cloths, ensuring that they were laundered each season and that there was an adequate supply of church candles.

View from a painting by the author

Van Gogh has painted wonderful scenes of meadows (with skylarks, sometimes) and I would love to have seen a painting of his of our very own one. I have several cards and pictures of the Vale church seen from the pond, complete with its bank of ochre rushes. But another view, accessible to all, is quite lovely. That is coming from what was Stampers shop, heading toward La Garenne.

I always wonder what visitors must make of this scene: the little bays and harbours with their boats bobbing in the blue sea to one side. On the grassy common yellow gorse and lupins flourish. In front the church resides majestically on its hill, somehow managing to have grandeur and simplicity at the same time and always, it seems to me, bathed in a soft light. To the other side, the nature reserve with an opportunity to view the wild birds without disturbing them.

When we were children our front room window looked directly toward the meadow gate. There was a deal more flooding in those days and sometimes, after much rain, the entire meadow, and those nearby, as far as Stafford Allen's house, would be under brackish water. This was, of course, before *le nocq* (the sluice) was cleaned and drained. We could see the grey and choppy tide slowly advancing toward the house. If it crept under the meadow gate and seeped into the approach path, with cottages and greenhouses either side. We were thrilled. We were going to be under water. It was like a tsunami about to swamp us.

Vale Pond, overlooked by the parish church, pictured in the 19th century

Outside and paddling about in the very cold and muddied water, my brother and I dared each other to go as close to the actual pond edge as we could. Our seaboots squelched, ankle-deep. You couldn't see where the pond bank began. The only clue was that the mud got softer and softer and we would pull back only if going further meant you would most likely end up at the bottom of the pond. It was quite disappointing when the water receded and everything went back to normal: a bit like watching a snowman melt.

The sound of the Vale Church bells echoing all around might mean people being called to a service. Or a wedding, or a funeral might be taking place. Both our children were christened there. Most of our family lie peacefully near the beaches and fields that they knew all their lives. Like the full circles of life and nature, there is something reassuringly complete and unchanging about the Vale church and its pond. Long may they both stay that way and continue to enchant us.

26 Finding Sanctus

December 2006

I came late to classical music and am still only in the shallowest of serious musical waters. A long time ago there was a certain television programme and I adored its background music so I contacted the BBC to find out what it was. It turned out to be Eric Satie's *Trois Gymnopedies* so I bought a version of this.

Again, watching my favourite film John Schlesinger's *Sunday Bloody Sunday*, I loved Mozart's trio *Soave sia il vento* from his opera *Cosi fan Tutte* which features throughout the film. If I ever had to choose records for *Desert Island Discs*, this would be firmly on the list.

Later, when studying for the Open University Eric Satie's music was analysed so I learnt a little more: about Satie's connection with Ravel and Debussy. A good friend who had a deep and wide knowledge of classical music told me that a good way of learning about this type of music is to try to identify the nationality of the composer, and the possible date of his compositions (yes, always a 'his', I'm afraid.) Very slowly, I found I could differentiate between, say, Tchaikovsky (Russian, 1840-1893) or Chopin (French, 1910-1849) and Elgar (English, 1857-1934) and that they were all termed 'Romantic' composers.

So, little by little, I have begun the wondrous journey of understanding and enjoying the most beautiful music known to mankind. Later, with the OU, we studied Mendelssohn's *Midsummer Night's Dream* and it was fun learning which notes signified the braying ass and which the entrance of the fairies. Next came Bach's *Brandenburg Concertos*, (German, Baroque 1720s – see I can even show off now) which I found exciting and inspiring. Gradually I realised that, far from being beyond my reach, classical music was very accessible and hugely enjoyable.

When St James concert hall was still an active church, my late mother-in-law used to be on the church committee and involved with St James' church bazaars. I well remember taking my own mother, Mary, to meet Kath for the first time at one of the Christmas bazaars, and how they immediately struck up a lasting friendship. And in those days, Elizabeth

College used to use St James church for all their school services.

Now, my husband Tony and I frequently attend St James concert hall to thoroughly enjoy both local and international stars. The standard of our local musicians and singers is quite ridiculously high and the musicians who are brought over are of staggering importance globally. Here, in our little Guernsey, we have sat mesmerised before the likes of Julian Lloyd Webber, Willard White and José Carreras – to name a few from a very long and distinguished list. And Guernsey audiences have been entertained, also, by top jazz stars – such as Ronnie Scott, Jamie Cullen and Madeline Bell. All of these have entertained in just the past few years.

One Sunday, the day after my father died, I drove along the coast by the Houmet du Nord. From there one can see over to the Vale Church, the L'Ancresse golf course, L'Islet and La Garenne, all places my father knew well from childhood. On the car radio I had Radio 3 on and the programme *Private Passions*. That Sunday the guest happened to be Sebastian Faulks, a writer whom I believe to be one of the greatest living novelists of our time (try reading *Birdsong* if you want to know what the soldiers of the First World War went through).

Faulks's choice included a composer I, in my faltering musical education, was not familiar with: the French composer, Fauré. As I drove along I found myself listening to the most sublime music I have *ever* heard. It was *Sanctus* from Fauré's *Requiem* and I will never forget hearing it for the first time.

Later, I thought *Sanctus* would have been a wonderful piece of music to be played at my father's funeral. Some time on, and by utter chance, I found myself looking at back numbers of the *Guernsey Press*. Astoundingly, I discovered that Fauré's *Sanctus* had been performed – by our local Concert Orchestra at St James – on the very Saturday night that my father died. So I like to think that he heard it, after all.

Not for the first time I felt a strong spiritual link between all the creative arts and faith. Now I have the New Philharmonia Orchestra version of the complete Fauré *Requiem* and play it again and again. And the Latin names from the Roman Catholic mass add, for me, a deep and significant meaning to the music.

What names they are: *Introit* – entrance; *Offertoire* – (offering); Sanctus – the angels tell us of the coming of Jesus: Holy, holy, holy; *Pie Jesu* – blessed Jesus; *Agnus Dei* – lamb of god; *Libera me* – deliver me; *In Paradisum* – in paradise. How timeless Latin words are – like the

*St James Church
Christmas Bazaar,
Guernsey, 1954*

The Duomo, Florence

Angelus – calling all to prayer; *Pieta* – any depiction of the Virgin Mary holding her son, the dead Christ, in her arms. *Pieta* doesn't mean piety but compassion and sorrow. And we know from the Latin mass: *Gloria in Excelsis* – Glory to God in the highest) and the *Credo* – a belief in God.

People are becoming curious about Latin again: see the bestseller book lists of 2006. And, as we celebrate Christmas Eve and maybe Midnight Mass, (some of us attending our only mass of the year) and then Christmas Day, we renew our faith. I believe music like Fauré's *Sanctus* helps us to meditate, lends us solace and a time to reflect on what mankind can achieve, with God's help.

Like Oscar Wilde said: 'One can exist without art, literature and music, but one cannot live without it.' I wish a happy Christmas to everyone, and a very peaceful New Year.

27 Alderney

September 2007

I am going to write about Alderney. It has at least three names: Alderney, Riduna and Aurigny. I have not visited our sister island (population 2,400), so, feeling clever, we book flights on the Internet. We are going to have a Sunday pub lunch in Alderney, explore the countryside and St Anne's, returning at 3.00pm.

Guernsey Airport, 8.00 am: it is foggy. But the fog lifts. Then it comes down again. Our flight is cancelled. The next flight, Guernsey to Alderney, will be at 1.30pm. We have to give up and go home.

In September we will try again. In the meantime, including some of Mr William Audoire's wonderful anecdotes, I proceed. Alderney, as do all her sister islands, has a very clear identity. Most badly hit by the German invasion of World War Two, Alderney's people must have been extraordinarily resilient, strong characters. They hold their 'Returning Day' on December 15th each year – it is their own, special, day. It is not quite the Liberation Day's of Guernsey and Jersey but one that encapsulates the rebuilding of their lives and bonding they have kept with their island over all these years.

Like those of the Guernsey Bailiwick and Jersey, Alderney people were advised to evacuate their island in 1940. The mass evacuation of around 1,400 folk left virtually nobody to look after property and so they returned to utter devastation. This was so bad that, by 1945, Alderney residents had to wait another six months after the May liberation of the other islands before returning to theirs.

As my parents found, in Guernsey much furniture had not been stored properly so that many things got mislaid. There was a sad loss of people's belongings and heirlooms. But, they rolled up their sleeves and got things going again. Everyone, as they said, was in the same boat. At least they had been spared witnessing the cruel atrocities inflicted by the German troops on prisoners of war. Alderney had, to all intents and purposes, been turned into a concentration camp.

As a child, people spoke to me of Alderney being flat and sandy.

I imagined a far off, windy place, with short, green grass. But as I researched and read more about Alderney I realize that it has a great deal more going for it than that. I would like to see the Sister Rocks, watch the Race of Alderney (a racing tide of 8 knots between the island and the Cotenin Peninsula of France), its unique wildlife and flowers.

The little town of St Anne's looks charming. Victoria Street is cobbled and I want to sample that pub lunch where they do not close on Sundays and are open all day, all year round. Heaven. Whilst in St Anne's I will buy an 'Alderney Time' clock: the numbers state '12ish, 1ish, 2ish…' We will visit Alderney Pottery and Channel Jumper, just because local endeavours are always more worthwhile.

Here are some of the customs and Norman laws the Ridunians (as Alderney people are known) kept and, possibly, still do.

'The first row of vegetables is for the public to take. The second for relations and the third and fourth to sell'

'All weeds in front of your house must by Law be removed by the end of May. Seawater is good for keeping weeds down.'

'You cannot light a bonfire on a Sunday.'

'All private pews in a Church must be cleaned and polished by the owners. No white lilies can be taken into a Church, not even at a wedding. All men must remove their hats. Women must wear a veil or cloth to cover their ears.'

'No child under 14 can be arrested for stealing fruit. Fruit is too tempting for a small brain.'

Mr Audoire told me he was born in 1925. Everyone knew each other and he was the youngest boy of five children. They had a working farm and each member of the family had jobs to do. His mother ran the farm and his father's job was as a quarry fireman: a 'dimity man'. Dimity is pop hole boring to 'bump' the face of the quarry, so giving the men enough stone to work on for the week. It was not blasting – for that could break the granite into pieces too small to working.

The senior Mr Audoire would be up at 5.30 and start the kettle up – kept free of limescale by keeping a small beach stone inside it. Then he would light large coppers for hot water and to wash the cows udders and tails. Then came the bread baking, tea and toast. Then he would be off to the quarry with a hunk of bread and a billy can of tea.

Mrs Audoire would then begin breakfast and prepare the children for school. Before that she would wash the cows tails and udders, in readiness for milking and taking them out to graze. One of the daughters would clean the oil lamps with soft hay and clip the wicks.

One brother kept 17 goats on the cliffs and often beheaded, gutted and skinned one or two for France for when the fishing boats left for Cherbourg. It is believed that the goat meat was passed off as deer, to get a better price.

As I remember my own Great Uncle Alfred had, Mr Audoire senior also had a best Sunday suit which he kept until he died. Later, in 1936, Mr Audoire took his dimity skills to Brecqhou to help build a house for a Captain Clark. So the family moved to Guernsey, in order that they all be together for the weekends.

My late father-in-law, Claude Ozanne, was a great Alderney fan. We have an Alderney great grandmother, Nancy, of the Duchemin and Mahé families, who married my great grandfather, Guernseyman Alfred Bréhaut.

We cannot wait to see Alderney now. In the meantime, our most northern Channel Isle has enjoyed a wonderful Alderney Week, a Wildlife Festival Weekend and I have the recipe for Milk-o-Punch. Chirri!

28 Alderney Visited

September 2007

Flying in an Aurigny plane is the closest you'll get to being a seagull and that is how it felt, winging over Alderney's south coast cliffs on a balmy late summer day. I look out of the window and see the rippling waves shimmer with gold over a misty blue sea, meeting the sky in unbroken blue cloud. We pass over Herm's Shell Beach and Oyster Point. Then the island of Alderney rises like a peaceful, sun-basking seal, entirely aware of how beautiful she is.

As we land at the airport I hear a cockerel crow: for me, a very good omen, boding well. In the airport all is friendly and unhurried. Eileen in the café offers us a cup of tea as though we are neighbours who have popped in for a chat. Well, I suppose that is actually true. The Aurigny pilot assists us to find our hire car representative, wishing us a good lunch and pleasant day. Our hire car lady good-naturedly complains about multinational procedures, as well she might. As we fill in her forms she assures us that if we have made a mistake, well, she'll give us a ring. So, not an anonymous, international airport but the friendliest, homeliest one you could imagine.

We begin our exploration with Braye Bay. It is much like our Pembroke and L'Ancresse, with wide sweeps of sand, ideal for children's bucket and spade holidays. We soon find Corblets Bay, with its pale yellow sand and a transparent green sea that reminds me of Guernsey's Jaonneuse Bay. That was, of course, before some clown decided it would be a good idea to dump all Guernsey's rubbish at Chouet.

By chance, we have visited all of the Channel Islands this year (except for Brecqhou and Jethou, but there's still time…) Joking apart, visiting idyllic Herm several times in summer is always a must. More unusually, we have been three times to Sark (I am becoming besotted) and also to Jersey to stay in our favourite, child friendly hotel. But, this is, ridiculously, for me a first time for Alderney. My husband remembers visiting when he was about 12. The photographs are of his mother, her sister and brother in 1911 on what looks to me like a fairytale holiday.

I expected wild and savage and got wild, yes, in the nicest possible way. Maybe 'untamed' would be a nicer word. But savage? No, indeed Alderney seemed a gentle place, recalling the quiet, northern end of Guernsey of my youth. Yet, the common land near the Hammond War Memorial did give me the shudders, like something very bad and sad happened there. One cannot help remembering the poor people who lost their lives during the German Occupation.

Alderney air has the cleanliness of Sark's. There is not much traffic, not even traffic lights (or filter system) and we saw a lot of people walking. They walked in twos and threes before and after Sunday lunch. They stopped to talk to each other like we used to do instead of driving past each other, muttering darkly, as we do now. The roads stretched ahead, as in our youth, with just one or two other vehicles to make way for now and then. Motoring bliss. Motoring as it was intended to be: to get you from place to place, not a mind-boggling nightmare that becomes worse every day. Our cars seem to get bigger and the drivers more impatient as each week goes by. Alderney inhabitants, by comparison, seem admirably sensible and drive mainly small cars.

St Anne's Victoria Street charm reminds me of Guernsey's Le Pollet, the Old Quarter and St Sampson's Bridge. Not brick for brick exactly, but the essential unhurried attraction of all those places. It helped that we had chosen a lovely, late summer Sunday. The cobbled street and houses were bathed in a soft light and St Anne's church bells peeled as we strolled down into the town. There is a well-attended service in progress but I am too shy to go in.

The Sunday papers have been delayed by the 'paper plane's' engine trouble. We know full well the frustration islanders feel when the Sunday papers, of all days, are not on sale. People were buying magazines they wouldn't normally dream of paying for and even taking Saturday leftovers. We recognize the disappointment. No newspapers is like having a lifeline cut off.

Lunch in the dappled garden of a Georgian building, and you could be eating *al fresco* in France. We sat in the sunny, still flowery terrace and I felt the springs of tension uncoiling. I let myself drift back to exactly this sort of pleasure: peace, warmth and a sense of well-being that I experienced with my great aunt when entertained in the traditional family houses of Guernsey. The place is lively but there is still a leisured, contented pace.

When I was a schoolgirl I used to roam around the back streets of

Guernsey's St Peter Port before getting the bus home. I'd nose around Burnt Lane, Pedvin Street and the hilly Mount Durand. In Alderney I had that same feeling of difference from the countryside of our islands. Of course Alderney is very French – the same France that Normandy presents. Yet the little island is plonk in the middle of the English Channel, which makes her quite unique and even more interesting.

I liked the lack of pretentiousness and the natural instinct of people to engage with their own society. Alderney hasn't been smartened up for visitors. It is itself, just like any self-respecting French village and we like it or lump it. I liked it very much and our next stay will be far longer.

I want to be woken up by a cockerel crowing. He'll live free range near the highly individual airport. You can see France clearly and I will buy that Alderney Time clock (deliberately vague as to the actual time) since the shop was closed this time around. But, as I said before, there are other days and the summer is not yet over.

29 Houmet Paradis

October 2004

Houmet Paradis: a tiny island, haven to our sealife. Long before Victor Hugo found it, Houmet Paradis was ours.

My father rented greenhouses at Houmtel, Vale, not far from Bordeaux. As a child I used to get mixed up with names, *Houmtel, Houmet du Nord, Houmet, Hougue* and *Sous les Hougues*. Yet they all mean small mounds, or promontories, and small, half-isles.

One day I had bunked off school, (it was double maths), and my father said that, as a penalty, I must help him in the greenhouses at the Houmtel. My job was the dreaded 'fertilizing', spreading the powdery yellow pollen of the young tomato plant with a 'fertilizer' (a stick with no more than some hen feathers nailed to a wooden rod).

Up and down the humid rows I plodded, wafting the fertilizer, smelling the peppery green leaves, downy with little white hairs. In the low front of the greenhouse I had to stoop low. It was like working in a green-tunnelled jungle. A bird flew in through the open lights and twittered angrily, trying to get out. I imagined that I was in some tropical forest, as the newly-watered earth rose in a light steam. Mud from the wet, earth paths soon caked my shoes.

Outside the sun shone hotly. Dad was in the small packing shed, reeling in the hose he had used to water each trough that the tomato plants grew in. We worked on until midday. I reached the last of the plants and threw open the greenhouse door. Fresh air filled my lungs and a light breeze cooled my face. I closed the wooden door behind me as fast as I could, as we had always been taught to do.

My father decided we would have a break. We would go to Bordeaux to see one of his friends, who had a small fishing boat moored there. It only took a few minutes and then he parked the lorry. We walked alongside the granite harbour wall.

Yes, there was Titch. He waved to us, calling out, 'Hey! Winno, mon viaer!' All Dad's friends had nicknames, like Ferpo, Big Wick, Little Wick and Beaver.

Titch, who wore a black eye patch (I never found out why) was bailing out some water from his boat and had some freshly dug lug-worms wriggling in a pail. The men made plans for a fishing trip the next Sunday. I could go, if I liked, with my sisters and brother. We would take crab sandwiches and fish for mackerel off Herm and Sark.

Leaving the men chatting, I left them to walk along the coast path, toward La Mielle. I loved La Mielle. Miss Leale lived there and she was my heroine because she had a white horse and won prizes at the gymkhanas. My friend and I used to ride our bikes over to La Mielle to try and get glimpses of her practicing in a field next to her house. (Since those days I have discovered that Miss Leale is now Jennifer Collas and an excellent artist.) It was then that I came to look more closely around this sandy area, near Houmet Paradis, although my brother and I had often cycled this way and fished near it.

Houmet Paradis, referred to in Victor Hugo's Toilers of the Sea

The sea was low, pebbles and boulders formed a grey bank over which Herm and Jethou sunbathed on the horizon. I could smell the wild chamomile and thyme. All around were granite rocks, set in the bracken-filled, tufty grass. My feet were damp from the greenhouse. The wind was cool now, blowing over the sea. Peewits and waders scuttled over the sand, gliding over the low tide, enjoying their meal. Gulls circled, high in the wide blue sky.

Then, there, asleep, just offshore, in Petils Bay, was Houmet Paradis. This day I sat on the yellow-lichened rocks, breathing in salt-air. Houmet Paradis beckoned and I longed to cross the exposed path of wet pebbles, strewn with glistening brown *vraic*. But I didn't have time. Dad would be already wondering where I was.

Perhaps, I thought, in our hearts we are all, still, *Toilers of the Sea*. Victor Hugo writes about this very spot in his book dedicated to the Guernsey people. Our island, and tiny isles like Houmet Paradis, are part of us, part of our very lives. I remembered a man who used to sleep overnight on Houmet Paradis, just for the joy of it. In the morning he woke to a clear dawn, gently lighting the islands, with the sound of the sea and the seabirds in his ears. The ferns and bracken smelt like aniseed and pine. Paradise, indeed.

With its teaming sealife, fishing, even sitting on the Herm ferry or rock-pooling, we cannot forget we are surrounded by the formidable beauty of our ever-changing and enchanting sea.

That day there wasn't a sound – no cars, no aeroplanes, save for the peewits and the oystercatchers. There was driftwood and a scattering of white shells. Little boats scurried by on the cerulean blue sea. Soon the mailboat would clear its majestic way toward St Peter Port harbour. Everywhere there were moorings, for this is a place of deep water, treasured by fishermen. Yet beware, I think to myself, of the strong and treacherous currents, this is no place for swimming. I love it all the more for not being tamed. Soon the tide will return and Houmet Paradis will be alone again, keeping its wildlife safe.

I walk back to Bordeaux harbour. There was no kiosk, public toilets nor car park. Dad is still talking to Titch, they are examining some crab-pots on the wet sand. They both wear seaboots, Dad because he has been watering in the greenhouse. Some little children play on the pier, collecting limpets for fishing for *cabots*, later on.

At last we go back to the lorry and return home. I think of Houmet Paradis. This fathomless, timeless place cannot be bought for money, not really. No more can anyone auction Guernsey. Because she is not for sale, and because she belongs to us.

30   Death of Our Market

June 2004

What shall we be most sad about, the death of dear old Mr Ben Gabriel, or the loss of our wonderful St Peter Port markets? Both, probably, and with equal dismay. Worse: I hear that there is talk of the markets being turned into a multi-storey car park. The two end facades would be kept, but in the middle would be the park. This would be an utterly criminal, seriously damaging act that would have a lasting effect on our island, not only on St Peter Port.

Gabriel's was one of the few clothes' shop in which my brother, who was profoundly deaf, felt at ease. Tozer's on the Bridge was another place he loved visiting for sweets and a newspaper.

Gabriel's always found Bruce's size, the colour and exactly the right garment. And they weren't always found straightaway. Not a bit of it. The assistants, often Mr Gabriel himself, went to endless trouble. The counter would soon be scattered with jeans and shirts as boxes were opened and shelves scrutinised.

Sometimes Mr Gabriel would rush around to one of his other shops, asking questions, getting help. He'd take things outside so you could see colours in daylight, then whisk items together to see if they matched. All this for a little lad who wouldn't be spending more than £10.

Down Fountain Street, the Gabriel shops face what is left of our poor Market. We used to go to the Market, buy fruit and meat for our mum. The stone floors in the fish stalls would be wet, the fish still alive, tails flapping. The smell was like the sea itself, seaweed dripping as the crabs crawled around, waiting to be bought.

There were dozens of Lady crabs (my favourite), spider crabs and chancre. Huge lobsters glared at you, antennae waving; sold three or four at a time to one family. They weren't a luxury then. And, in the meat halls, there'd be sawdust and the unforgettable smell of beef, marbled with creamy fat, hanging on hooks. "What'll it be today, madam?" our butcher would say, sharpening his steel cleaver. On a scrubbed board he'd chop, tenderise, then weigh your joint, giving you exactly how you wanted it. Often you came away with more than you thought had needed – the home-made sausages and readymade mince and paté looked so good.

Flowers were only for a treat for us, freshly picked, perfect in their cool buckets. You could choose one stem from each bucket, if you wanted. Then the fruit: select one orange as you wished, and a bunch of thyme or watercress. Everything was so tempting. Stall holders always had a word or two for you. Very often the produce had been grown by them. Shopping was an occasion.

Celebration for King George V, 1911

At Christmas we always shopped at the Market. Now, soulless supermarkets sell soulless 'festive' food and pre-wrapped, glitter-spattered decorations so tacky and garish they make my head ache.

After we had shopped, you might pop over and change a library book at Guille-Allès. The building, so cool and quiet was a haven from the bustle outside. You'd sit on a window seat and browse through a book before borrowing it. Outside the window was a view of the Market, with people going in and out of its grand façade.

Out in the sun again and you could go up Mill Street to Leale's to look at the kitchen utensils and china, making notes of what you might like if you got married. Years ago you could smell the vegetables at Vaudin and Keates. I never go to the Bordage without thinking of them. Then, perhaps, a cup of tea at the little café – there is still one there – by the French Halles.

Up Mansell Street and on to Trinity Square, so like the old quarters retained by the French. And, in seaside places like Vannes, in southern Brittany, you can still stroll through a jostling, inhabited town, its narrow, twisted streets, just like ours, thronged with life. People drink coffee and sip wine at tables outdoors, under coloured canopies, with shopping at their feet.

And I still think that if I climb the hundreds of steps I'll get to The Little Theatre. After a show, still with the play on my mind, we'd walk down them again, my mother and I, in the dark and we would chatter all the way to the bus terminus. The Market would be quiet then, like a keeper of all that is good, ready to open early to the bustle of the Saturday trade.

If you went the other way, down the market steps and the square in front of the Town Church, you could see the Market, Gabriel's, and Guille-Allès library. Close neighbours, they are like old friends.

The Market is the hub of the old part of town, a local haunt, just as the Bridge belongs to Guernsey people. Even Cornet Street and Hauteville won't seem the same if the Market is finally destroyed. It is the core of and was the first residential area of St Peter Port.

St Peter Port itself a gem to be jealously guarded, surely. And the wonderful Church is of the utmost historical value. If anything, it should be surrounded by more pedestrian precincts, not yet more cars. Incidentally, isn't the whole point of building all these new flats, where our Hotels used to be, that they are within one hop from offices in Town? Yet the most expensive ones all have garages! So the States of Guernsey are talking about getting rid of the glorious Market and replacing it with a car park.

Who said the States of Guernsey can do this? Why haven't islanders been consulted? I know, personally, that Mr Ben Gabriel was a generous, morally conscious man. He and his heirs have steadfastly kept to their values and their way of doing things. Guernsey people must be allowed to do the same, it is our heritage and our right.

It is not too late. The potential to do something very special with the Market site is still there. In Guernsey we have already paid far too high a price to the motor car: loss of peace and beauty.

Destruction of our very lovely Town of St Peter Port and of our island really does have to stop. Right here, and right now.

31 Babis's Apples

November 2008

Funny old world, isn't it? One minute there we are coveting our rich neighbour's orchards and the next we are all, including the neighbour, scouring the earth for any windfalls we can find for food. Apparently, there is a 'Credit Crunch'. Not that it makes much difference to us since we never did have much credit for crunching or even secretly storing.

Greed by the few has almost done for us all and it is going to take some safe hands, cool heads and strong nerves to get us through. The generation of 'gimme, gimme, gimme' and the woeful, wilful waste of the world's resources are waking up to what is, for the post-war generation, a very familiar story of make do and mend. One almost feels sorry for the 'loadsamoney' lot. For the first time, they are suddenly having to stop in their tracks and think about job security, financial ruin, threatening mortgages, reduced pensions and worrying school fees. Then there is the private health scheme to be paid for and as for bonuses…

Welcome to our world. In the forties and fifties our situation was much the same. It was a bleak outlook for those returning to a devastated island. People lost their furniture, businesses had disappeared, many houses needed renovation and their gardens replanted and re-landscaped.

Wherever you could you grew your own vegetables and fruit. Every spare bit of land had its chickens and pigs. Men, young and old, knew how to shoot rabbits and fish for the family table. Fires weren't lit until the evening. Logs were hewn to save on coal. Central heating was unheard of.

Women used to darn their stockings, knit woollens, sew and bake. Leftovers were carefully saved and used for pies, stocks and soups. This wasn't always, as I recall, because women wanted to be housewives particularly. I can recall many a grandmother and great aunt who preferred to read, walk, use her creative abilities, socialise and do other things more precious to her time. It was a question of having to do it, like it or not.

Schools had scant materials at the beginning of island recovery. At the Vale Infant School in 1946 we had to roll plasticine into the shapes

Family allotment, 1920s

of letters and numbers on a cork board. You scraped the stuff off next day and used it again. It went an interesting colour over the days (usually purple) and mine, anyway, collected additional hair and other bits of I know not what. Many teachers had returned from evacuation, so were themselves having to readjust to an island life much changed. A lot of women were virtually single or widows, with men either killed during the war or still on active service in the forces.

It was seen as very shameful if a man relied on what is now called social benefits. In fact, in Guernsey in the forties, such benefits as there now are, didn't even exist. There were those, of course, as there are in any parish, who needed to be assisted. There always will be folk who cannot cope. That was, and is, understood.

Because of society's need for a strong family unit, women who had babies out of wedlock, divorcees and gay men and women were largely stigmatised. They were judged as weakening the family ideal, and thus society, so were made social outcasts. These people and their babies had a hard time of it – enduring much unnecessary and, especially by today's tolerance, unheard of isolation and derision.

In the main, people buckled down and coped. Slowly, with farmers, family-run shops and businesses, with tomato and flower growing small-holdings, all run with family help, the island began to flourish as we eased out of financial restrictions. My parents worked seven days a week with just a few days off in the autumn. This was the norm throughout the island and, indeed, the Channel Islands. Children helped out when they got home from school.

We always used the buses since hardly anyone had cars. We never had foreign holidays. One winter coat saw you out for many years. New shoes were bought only when the others had worn out. Plastic bags, black sacks, silver foil, cling film and kitchen rolls hadn't been invented. You returned your glass bottles to the shop for a refund. Vegetables, with muddy roots, were put into your basket unwrapped.

How strange it is going to seem to some people if they have to cut down on travel – I get internet offers of up to 70% off cruises and package holidays for not much more than my monthly wine bill. Well, okay, that might not be a very good example, but you get the idea, I am sure.

Our first mortgage (only possible because we lived with my in-laws for two years, literally saving every penny we could for the deposit) crippled us for ten years. In 1961 we bought a semi-detached house with no bathroom and an outside lavatory. The kitchen had nothing in it but a sink. It took time to fit things out with lots of DIY. In the meantime, we had two children and our first holiday was a week in a bed and breakfast (Castle View) in Jersey. The children saved their pocket money to buy one toy each and they both remember that holiday as the best they ever had. So do we. We were in our early thirties.

Recently we had a quite delicious, reasonably priced meal. It was all home-cooked. In fact the owner told us that the apple pie I had just eaten (mouth-watering) was made from apples picked from his back garden. There was a roaring fire in a fireplace surrounded by comfortable chairs. It was November 8th but fireworks sprayed and sparkled over the black sky of St Peter Port harbour. For once, I didn't complain (it was not November 5th – yes, I agree, that is quite another story) but I sat back and enjoyed Babis's apples. If this is the future, then maybe a 'Credit Crunch' is not all bad and maybe, in the long run, it may even do us all a great deal of good.

32 Get Fresh

January 2009

' Get Fresh with Guernsey Toms' went the slogan, complete with a cupid's arrow slicing through it, a nice hint at the tomato as a love apple. This was when the Guernsey Tomato Marketing Board existed in the 1960s and '70s. Recently some friends sent us a recipe booklet, produced by Good Housekeeping, no less, and the GTMB, in 1970. It is about our then much in demand Guernsey tomatoes.

Our friends were with Kenilworth Vineries. They have gone on to tour the world with ICARDA (International Centre for Agricultural Research in Dry Areas). They improve the welfare of poor people through research and training in dry areas of the developing world by increasing the production and nutritional quality of food. ICARDA preserve and improve a given area's resources with essential crops like durum wheat (used for pasta), chickpeas, barley, lentils and the fava (broad) bean. These crucial foods can be grown in very dry countries albeit with a careful watch on the use of water.

As we become embroiled in an unheard of economic turmoil, maybe the time has also come when we can make changes to affect our own lives. Those of us who were brought up by food producers (our tomato growing ancestors), farmers and fishermen, have a strong oral history of Guernsey culture and her environment. We know about our own food traditions – which crops grow best in which part of the island; that parsnips are sown in deeply trenched soil in January, mackerel is plentiful off Herm's coast. We were taught which rocks and where to search for ormers.

As children we heard our grandparents talking about the difference certain wind directions and tides made, the soil, months and seasons. 'Christmas on the doorstep (sitting in the sun), Easter with the poker (sitting near the fireplace).'

We know that we are still permitted to gather vraic for fertilizer. *Point de vraic, point de hautgard* (no sea-weed, no stack yard – a yard kept for harvests of hay). The best months for *vraic* gathering are June, July and August. Dry seasons are bad for the growth of sea-weed, because it

Above: Edwin Bréhaut, 1928

Right: Claude Ozanne, 1926

Claude's greenhouse in Rue Perrot, 1926

121

needs rain just as the grass does. So, turning to locally grown food, even to growing our own vegetables and fruit will be neither a novelty nor a fear for us.

As well as shopping at market gardens and hedges for our vegetables and fruit, allotments for rental exist. Some supermarkets are now willing to accept and sell fresh, local produce. We mustn't lose too many of our fields purely for leisure. Recently I learnt that, in England, because of European Union edicts, some farmers are paid not to farm by their government. So they rent out their land to caravan and boat owners as dry dock. Meanwhile another fast food eatery is allowed. That is not just sad that is insanity.

Interestingly, not so long ago, land workers left for employment in towns, became involved with – and some instrumental in forming – trade unions, changing the workers' way of life forever. Now, some of those seeking to escape what has become the modern, faster life are trying to return to the land, only to find how much we have come to rely on massive supermarkets that dictate not only what is sold, but what is grown.

In some countries like the developing sub-Sahara of South Africa, the poor are given no choice but to adapt to ever more brutal standards, whilst those working on a stock exchange rule like feudal Lords. The chasm between those with obesity problems and those starving is grotesque. In such circumstance, people have lost their land and the right to grow food for their families. But, in today's global economic crisis, it isn't so much that those with the power to should shift to local production of food: it is that they must.

Is it any wonder that programmes such as *Lark Rise to Candleford* are so popular? They remind us of days of chivalry, of lost values and good manners. This economically poorer, kinder, culture is closely linked to people living from the soil with their local knowledge and country traditions. It is called quality of life.

Those who dismiss the film *Mamma Mia!* as lightweight completely miss the point of why it is so popular. To millions the film portrays an island life where people struggle to survive, yes. But the story shows that they can succeed without great wealth and in the meantime live in a close community in a warm climate.

In the book about Guernsey Toms, it says: 'In the region of 115 million pounds of tomatoes are grown each year'. Those really were the days, weren't they? It goes on to describe the tomato industry and how we grew our crops in Guernsey greenhouses.

Here is one of the rather charming recipes given:

Pork L'Ancresse

Serves 4

4 pork chops, 1 oz butter, 2 oranges, 1lb Guernsey tomatoes, sliced. 2oz onion peeled and diced, 2tbspn vinegar, 1tbspn dark brown sugar, half tspn dried basil, 1 clove garlic, peeled and crushed. Half lb long grain rice.

Brush chops with melted butter, grill for 10mins. Take 4 slices orange plus rind and juice of one. Add toms, onion, vinegar, sugar, grated orange rind, juice, basil and garlic to grill pan. Grill for 30mins. Cook rice. Arrange chops on rice, thicken juices in pan, pour over chops. Garnish with orange slices.

Quite why this should be called 'Pork L'Ancresse' it doesn't say, but it is delicious. Another recipe called 'Guernsey Quiche' is the same as any other quiche recipe but using only Guernsey tomatoes. Well done the GTMB of yesteryear for an excellent promotion.

Anyway, our soil is still the same and so is the quality of our sunlight and temperatures. Surely we can still grow crops of our good old Guernsey Toms? We probably won't, ever, see the return of an island proud to be growers, taking even greater pride in our care of Guernsey's environment and of her islanders. But we can try.

33 Adèle Hugo

For some time I had been looking for a studio to paint in. I needed quiet and space. My then boss, a kindly Oxford man, smiled at me one day. 'I know just the place,' he said, 'But it must be a secret. You are not to tell anyone.' Why? Because the room he had in mind was in Hauteville House, owned by Paris.

At first I said no, Hauteville House was far too grand! But he persisted. 'I know the housekeeper. She'll let me have keys. But no-one must know. Paris would not be amused.'

I could understand that. But his offer was tempting. So, after a frustrating painting weekend, when telephones rang and dogs ran in and out of my corner of the kitchen, I asked my boss to find out more about the proposed studio for me.

At length, it was arranged that I would take my paints, easel and canvases and gain entrance by a side door, by pre-arrangement. It was all very exciting and I much looked forward to producing something worthwhile in this renowned literary home of Victor Hugo.

As I arrived a side door creaked open and the house-keeper beckoned me inside. Immediately I felt a chill of foreboding. I wore a long black coat with a hood trimmed with black fur. The housekeeper jangled her bunch of keys as we mounted the polished wooden stairs. Our footsteps echoed around the hall. All was quiet. Under my arm I grasped my little holdall of equipment. My heart began to race.

As we climbed upward, I glanced at Victor Hugo's strange artefacts, his glass floor and carved furniture. This was where the great man had written *Toilers of the Sea*, dedicated to Guernsey. In this house his family lived out their exile from Paris, as Victor Hugo, with his forthright republican views, had left them no choice.

But Hugo loved Guernsey, loved the view from his lofty studio of the smaller islands and the coast of France itself. Not so his long-suffering wife and children who yearned to return to mainland Europe.

We stopped on the landing and the housekeeper unlocked a heavy wooden door. Inside was a room with windows overlooking Hauteville hill. The long lace curtains were scarcely drawn, only permitting a sliver of light. There was a chandelier in the middle of the ceiling, dusty and unlit. Another closed door led to an adjacent room.

"Please do not make any mess," said the housekeeper, "and you may not exceed two hours. I will wait downstairs." I nodded, thanking her for her trouble and kindness in allowing me to be here at all. She gave me a stern look and I wondered if my boss had perhaps twisted her arm a little too painfully?

She left, closing the door behind her. I lay down newspapers and set up my easel. I selected brushes and poured out linseed oil and turpentine into little tin tubs. The tubes of paint were laid out and I selected the colours I wanted and began to mix some on my palette. I thought I might begin a self-portrait. Where would I put my mirror?

Then, just as I applied my first brushstroke there was an enormous WHOOSH of energy, landing in a thump on my back. It nearly knocked me over. Horrified, I turned around to see the window open and the curtains flapping madly in a sudden gale. My newspapers lifted off the floor and I had to grab my easel to stop it falling over.

Again, I felt small fists beating my back and heard, "Get out! Get out! Get out!" But there was no-one else in the room! The sky darkened, it became icy cold and I could barely see. Without hesitation I stuffed all my belongings back into my bag. Shaking with fear I dismantled my easel. In my terror I left the newspapers skittering around the floorboards. A last ferocious push and I was outside on the landing. Behind me the door blew shut with a loud bang.

Instantly the light came back and the wind ceased. I ran down the stairs, clattering and trembling. Where was the housekeeper's room? I couldn't find it. I ran from door to door, yelling, "Let me out! Help!"

The housekeeper came running up to me, "For heaven's sake. Stop making such a noise. You'll waken the dead."

"Dead? Whose dead?" I mumbled, making a beeline for the door to Hauteville hill.

"Why, they all are now," she replied.

"The Hugo family? Yes, I know. Whose room was I in?" I asked, breathing in huge gasps of cool air as I stood outside on the pavement.

"Adèle Hugo's," said the housekeeper. "You were in Adèle Hugo's room."

Some days later my boss looked sternly at me, over his pince nez spectacles. "That was such an opportunity. I went to great trouble for you."

I apologized to him for not taking the 'studio' and tried to explain. He merely shook his head. "You have always had such an imagination!"

Yes, I have. He was right. But Adèle Hugo intrigued me. Why was she so vehemently against me using her room? Why was she so angry? Well, I think I now know the answer.

Adèle Hugo was a gifted musician. But in her day, in mid-nineteenth century France she was expected only to marry, and to marry well. She was cruelly restricted. Centuries of French custom forbade unmarried women, or those who were under 25, the age of majority, from even appearing in public unescorted. Under French law Victor Hugo was well within his rights to confine his daughter to her room for a month or more if she crossed his wishes.

And Adèle Hugo did argue and rail against her exiled imprisonment. To make thing worse, she fell passionately in love with a man who didn't want her. As Adèle tried to live freely, and not be a chattel, a man's possession, she began, slowly, to lose her mind. Eventually leaving Guernsey, by tricking her parents, she followed her love, Alfred Pinson, to Canada and then Barbados. All the while her high position in life and her Parisian lifestyle began to slip away.

At least her brother, François-Victor saw to it that Victor Hugo sent his errant daughter a regular allowance, and François always managed to keep track of her.

But by the time Adèle Hugo returned to France she was judged insane and Victor Hugo had her committed to an asylum. She remained there, even after Hugo's death, for the last thirty years of her life.

So, I now understood why an unfulfilled young woman beat me out of her room. The shame is that I, too, wanted to use my gift, my painting skills which I never, fully, have. Perhaps in another life we might meet and share some thoughts.

One evening, years later, we were having a quiet drink at the Royal Hotel. A noisy group arrived at the bar, with great fanfare and excitement. It was Francois Truffaut the French director and the actress, Isabelle Adjani, with the film crew and hangers on. They had been filming *Adèle H*, in Guernsey, Adèle Hugo's life story.

I glanced at the darkly beautiful Isabelle and wondered if she was anything like Adèle Hugo. Perhaps. But she could not, possibly, be as intriguing, romantic and as tragically wasted as Adèle.

Even now, when I visit Hauteville House with visiting friends, Adèle's door remains resolutely unwelcoming. I still feel the pressure from the room behind. I can still hear, "Get out! Get out! Get out!"

I will, Adèle, never again invade your troubled privacy. Your spirit has earned its freedom. What's more you have gained my understanding and admiration. Let this year be the year Adèle Hugo is also remembered, for her courageous stand against her father's domination. And for the lonely and exiled years she spent in Guernsey, in Hauteville House.

Tragic daughter of Victor Hugo, Hauteville

34   Vive La Différence

August 2004

Everyone, it seems to me, is going to France for their holidays. Some have houses or apartments there, some caravans, some are going in their boats. Some will holiday in style in grand hotels. Some will tour in their 'People Movers'. We are going to a self-catering *gite* in Brittany. There, we can visit the early morning markets and shop for lunch.

Of course we had visited France when we were young (always by boat, we never flew). But for our first French family holiday, we shared a dormobile, called *Freda*, plus a leaky tent. To us this was really going abroad and extremely exciting.

Our parents and grandparents never took "annual holidays". The expression, "Where are you going for your main holiday?" didn't exist. We didn't take main holidays, never mind weekend breaks or having a holiday allowance for three or more holidays a year. We never thought of going to such places as far-flung cities and Europe, and certainly not of trips taking many hours of flight.

Our hardworking ancestors were busiest in the summer, toiling literally dawn till dusk. Come the autumn, they might take two or three days off and we'd go to Sark, say, or Jersey if we had the money. And these would be treasured family days when Dad came too (because he was usually so busy). We would all dress up in our best. 'Lunch' out was a huge treat, even though we actually called it dinner-time. Lunching out informally was neither fashionable nor catered for by restaurants. To buy something you could really cook yourself was considered the height of indulgence.

As for hotels: I thought they were just for weddings and for visitors when they came to Guernsey. I first stayed in a hotel in London, the Strand Palace, when I was sixteen. I accompanied my father on a business trip – he had to visit Covent Garden; he was a commission agent for tomato and flower growers. My brother, then aged twelve, went to a school for the deaf in Margate and was travelling up by train to London. Then we would take him home with us.

At the Strand Palace, it was breakfast and an intimidating waiter came round with some things I had never seen before, in a basket. He held a pair of tongs, expectantly. I had no idea what was going on. "You're supposed to choose a roll," said my exasperated father. "Oh!" I said and duly obliged. Then I buttered the thing and stuttered out what I wanted to eat from the printed menu. I found the whole exercise extremely embarrassing and couldn't wait to get out of the dining room.

But it was fun having my own bedroom with its own toilet and washbasin and – good gracious, a bath! We had an outside toilet at home. Since our hot water was heated via a coal-fuelled Raeburn, it was usually tepid. I thought The Strand Palace was very posh, and I remember that London visit to this day.

Pembroke, 1930. Note absence of sea walls

But, back to France: *Freda* the dormobile was a sturdy old girl and she took us from St Malo up as far as Lisieux in Normandy and right down to Pont Aven in Brittany. We stayed at campsites, taking turns to share the tent. During an horrendous storm we soon found out that the tent leaked and that our sleeping bags were not waterproof. There were clothes washing facilities at the campsites and dodgy showers you could take, after buying tokens. You had to wash *tout de suite*, though, or the water would run out before you had rinsed your hair.

But the countryside was lovely and the food divine. Each village had its own patés and cheeses, bread, milk and wine. I fell deeply in love with the country and remain so still. But France did test us. We knew little French then and being 'abroad' was quite challenging and foreign. As so today, in some areas, French people didn't go out of their way to speak any English. Although we shared the driving, it was tiring when you are not used to driving on the right. And we got mixed up with the francs. And the toilets were sometimes no more than a hole in the ground. Reached, sometimes, by a long queue you had to try really hard to stay loving this country and its way of life.

Happily, we got to see places like Bayeux, Mont St Michel, Quimper and Pont Aven (which Gauguin, among other painters, made famous) and the children learnt a little French. In fact this trip whetted their appetite and they also came to find France a delightful refuge.

Still, it was many years later before we went further afield, to the Mediterranean, where young people now hop over to as though it were Herm. Now, we visit France several times a year. I know of people who almost commute on a regular basis. One couple have a place near the Alps, because they love to ski. Others, go as far south as possible for the climate. Some prefer only an hour's drive (no more) from St Malo or Dinard: for others it has to be Rennes with the fast train to Paris and EuroDisney. Several, some quite young, friends have left Guernsey to live permanently in France.

Nonetheless, in my youth, our afternoons off with maybe no more than a walk around Pleinmont and an ice cream were all we wanted. And I can recall picknicking between the grassy slopes opposite Pembroke, before the golfers pretty well claimed that tufty green common land. Just being together was all that counted, having family times in our sunny little island. We would chat to other families, themselves all eating *al fresco*. It was a real social outing.

Guernsey was slowly recovering from its war-inflicted wounds. People were back from afar, not ready to be travelling off again so soon. Those who stayed during the Occupation were just glad to be part again of the longed for peaceful times in their island. Who needed foreign holidays? Everything we wanted was all around us.

Those were the days, my friends. We thought they'd never end. Yet, it seems France has managed to keep many of her traditions and attractions. Why can't we?

35   Of Clams and Camping

September 2005

The French, of course, have a word for it: Rentrée. In September we 're-enter' our normal world. For two months or more the fortunate ones amongst us have been on holiday. We have vacated our usual positions and gone off – taken a break and gone away.

But, come September and the drawing in of the evenings we must enter the real world again, of school terms, assembly of government and commerce.

Autumn brings both harvests gathered in from the rapidly passing year and also sees us gearing up for the winter, and, well before January, a new year.

For a few summer weeks we have escaped the harnesses and fetters of schoolroom, office and debating chamber. We are reined in by society's structures that govern our social strictures. We are surrounded by the rules and regulations that keep us tame and in place.

What bliss, then, are the summer holidays. It is July and we are off: kicking over the traces and running free. Just for a few days we become families again – picnicking, fishing and holding get-togethers. Sometimes we meet up in far-off lands and unfamiliar territories, feeling the sand between our toes and the hot sun warming our backs.

This past week I saw family group after family group climbing down a wet and windy cliff path in Brittany. There was a spring tide, much like ours, and all the locals were armed with buckets, rakes, forks and iron hooks. They swarmed over the wide and sandy bay. Small children in seaboots ran hand-in-hand with their grandparents to special, secret spots for the best catch.

We saw a grandfather take his little grandson of around eight years and scramble down steep steps and over sharp brown rocks. What were they looking for? I asked in hesitant French.

"Les palourdes grises", said the old man.

Later, in the *gite*, I looked the words up and discovered that they had been hunting grey clams. I had watched the absorbed pair through my

Lamballe, Britanny

Camping in Herm

binoculars. They walked, in misty grey drizzle, until they were but specks in the distance. Then they disappeared over a sand bank. What a feed they must have had!

We guessed that the nets were for langoustine and the hooks for conger-eel. Indeed, in all the fishmongers and harbour stalls next day were fresh catches and the clams were like cockles but great round ones and twice the size.

But the family involvement took me back again to when my uncles, aunts and cousins all met up with us on the beaches of Guernsey. We just naturally formed groups.

We were in and out of each other's houses then. Aunts would pop round on their bicycles, with baskets in the front holding purchases from the corner shop. They just wanted a chat, for no particular reason. The social bonding was invisible but strong and went back generations.

France has retained this. On the beaches the older generations are included as they sit sedately on foldable chairs, under sun umbrellas. Teenagers join them, kissing their elders on both cheeks. Cousins and friends shake hands cordially then embark on long discussions about goings on and plans for the future. It is quite delightful to see.

I took my two granddaughters camping for a week in Herm this July. I wanted them to see how beautiful unspoilt island life can be. We went bird-watching, each with our binoculars, sketch pads and cameras. We saw different kinds of seagull, cormorant, fulmars, oyster catchers and – we think – an egret.

I showed them the wildflowers, butterflies and insects. We strode around the cliff paths, bordered by thick green bracken, up and down the slippery and stony paths. It was hot and hard work but very rewarding.

One night it rained and we thought the wind might take the tent off, like a kite. The girls, though, were unafraid and said that it was exciting – like being in a film about make-believe (we had seen *Charlie and the Chocolate Factory* and they love *Harry Potter*). The younger granddaughter thought our tent was a cross between a spaceship and the Tellytubby house.

Over the sunny fields we could see Guernsey and St Peter Port, where the girls live. Sark looked glorious and next time we camp we will get a tent on the slopes overlooking the clear blue sea to that island. From Herm all the familiar landmarks are seen at a different angle. Jethou, Brecqhou, Alderney and France all held an unusual picture for our cameras.

We hiked over the quiet fields, where baby calves grazed on lush grass, (we named them all and visited them each day, even sketching them,) we looked at St Sampson's. The girls could see quite clearly now how Guernsey sloped from Jerbourg, St Martin's, to the Vale and the Northern end of Guernsey.

After that, we slid down the dusty, tree lined path to Belvoir Bay and swam in crystal-clear sea (no it wasn't cold, just 'refreshing'). We had the beach to ourselves at eight in the morning and that is when we think we saw the egret.

So, away from it all, a change is as good as a rest. But then, come September and back to the real worlds of academia, of life indoors and making a living. We are ready though, for this routine, for the touchable boundaries that make complete freedom so pleasant, desirable and necessary.

Ahead are the time-worn customs and celebrations that cultures have all built for themselves. We have a reason for it all, a sense of place and a sense of season on God's good earth.

'Rentrée': we are back and preparing to move forward. Ahead lies new seedlings on cleansed land. The children have new school uniforms, pens and pencil cases. We are seeing what life might bring us once more, in this – our own little corner of the world.

36 French Exchange

August 2008

As children in the 1940s we pottered about, exploring Les Amarreurs' small piers. France might as well have been Australia, it seemed so far away. In fact, when we were very young, even Bordeaux harbour seemed a long way off to me. Our mainland in those days was definitely England (not 'Britain' as such). Most of the world, Europe in particular, was recovering from World War Two. So devastated, especially northern, France was not an obvious place for holidays or weekend breaks in those days.

Even getting to Jersey seemed to take hours and there wasn't even a regular service to St Malo. We wouldn't have dreamt of flying to France even if the link to Dinard existed then, which I don't think it did. Of course, once we did get a taste for France we have never wanted to stop.

Now, we count several French families amongst our friends and attended the wedding of our daughter's French exchange. The charming ceremony was held in St Briac. Corinne, her mother and family visited us this summer. We couldn't believe that we had known each other for thirty years. Soon, my daughter and Corinne's children will enjoy their own exchange, continuing a delightful link for us all.

Like many Guernsey people, now we are familiar with places like Normandy, Brittany, the Loire, Provence and even Paris. What a country France is with so many contrasts. What a lot we missed out on all those years ago.

Our Norman roots have, if anything, strengthened over the years. Caen University is attended by students wanting to become Guernsey Advocates. Norman law is taught at the University – in French – so our would-be Advocates are baptised, as it were, early on in their careers with a strong dose of Norman-French history. Guernsey men and women are proud to have northern French blood coursing through their veins.

Now that we live in St Peter Port, I see the older part of town: grand town houses mingled with terraced, slate-roofed and modest residences. But all are built on the same sunny hill that slopes down to our beautiful

Above: Alison, Corinne, Yvonne and Michael in London, 1978.

Right: The Drouin Chateau, where Corinne and Fransesc held their wedding reception

Below: Corinne's marriage to Fransesc, 1997

harbour. It is as good as any in Europe.

From our window the view is dominated by the graceful green spire of St Joseph's Roman Catholic church. Beyond that is a sliver of sea, changing every day from deep blue to silver depending on wind and cloud. We can see a little bit of Sark and even Jersey on a clear day. You can see these islands from Bordeaux, of course, but from here, oddly, they seem to be a bit grander and more glamorous.

In the town itself, are our market halls. I understand we needed to upgrade the building but couldn't we have kept a little of it just as it was? Recently we sat to have coffee in the cold, stone hall with its walls towering toward a windowed ceiling. I realised that on this very spot Guernsey people once sold their home-grown produce and remembered the bustling scene of years ago. In France, every small town and village has its market. They are more than commercial outlets – they are meeting places for gossip and news. They are vibrant, full of colour and culture. I left my coffee cup half full and fled.

At least home-grown produce can be bought from local shops and from the Saturday Farmers' Markets. The *Viaer Marchi* and our shows are still alive and kicking and they still have a lot of lively fun about them. All the seafood and floral festivals are simply wonderful. So we mustn't be too downhearted.

It was intriguing to see that such esteemed publishers as Bloomsbury chose to launch their book *The Guernsey Literary and Potato Peel Pie Society* (yes, I have bought it but yet to read it. It certainly looks very interesting) in the St Peter Port market square. Our food, such as Guernsey gâche and bean jar were on offer.

They are substantial dishes, but not, though, as robust as some French fare. Here is a recipe for a Provençal dish:

8 thrushes,
8 slices of bread, butter, seasoning
Pluck the thrushes, cover in butter, thrust a skewer through the birds and roast them at high temperature.
Place the bread below to recover the faeces...

Um, well I think not, don't you?

In October we are going to Cape Town, South Africa. We will visit the thriving vineyards there. In 1688 thousands of French Huguenots fled to the Cape. Through industry and skill they soon established the flourishing wine producing area. The place we are going to visit is called *Franschhoek* (French Corner) and, since you ask, the renowned Rickety Bridge vineyard.

Today countless South Africans have French names but do not speak French. Places like Basse Provence and Rochelle were named after the country that I am sure the Huguenots very much missed. It will be fascinating to learn more about the Huguenots and to make the connection between our own Guernsey and French family history.

We have all come a long way from Les Ammareurs and the shelter that that small harbour gave us as Guernsey slowly recovered from German occupation. To us, Pleinmont and indeed all of the south cliffs were a long way off. It would have meant taking two buses to see them – one to town, one to the bay. Quite expensive with a bit of planning needed. Our busy parents, growing their tomato crops, didn't have time for such things. What was wrong with the beach nearest to you?

Already our children and grandchildren have seen far more of the world than we ever did, or probably will. Their adventures grow ever more sophisticated. Like California, Europe Disneyland, the Caribbean and the Mediterranean and they have been to Prague, Copenhagen, Berlin and Florence. Their French exchange will include Barcelona where Corinne now lives with her Spanish husband, Francesc.

I do envy them. Though I wouldn't swap the Guernsey we knew. No, not for anything.

37 Venice with Nina and Kate

May 2004

Three old friends, Kate, Nina and me, go way back to the 1960s in Guernsey. *Take Three Girls* (which we all liked) was a TV serial. Liza Goddard, Angela Down and Susan Jameson starred. It was something we identified with, in those days – three young women wanting so much to fulfil our potential – three people, wondering what life held. Now all in our own sixties, we decided on a few days reunion in Venice. Kate and Nina now both live in England.

Arriving via Stansted and Treviso we jumped on a waterbus – a kind of Herm ferry that the locals use exactly as buses. It was late evening and we hit commuter rush hour. Venetians have a determined air and sharp elbows, so we, with all our luggage, and not knowing where we were going, were – distinctly – in their way. We soon learnt the knack of boarding and disembarking, and also that waterbuses' arrows show where they have come from, not where they are going to. "Venetians," we agreed, "do it backwards!"

So we arrived in Venice by dark sea, rippled with the lights of the harbour. Very intriguing. The hotel was wonderfully central but, well, 'basic' is the most polite word. Kate had made the bookings, practical as ever, and was soon our map-reader. Nina was chief 'euro guard' and I became cultural guide.

Venice has myriad little squares (*compos*) where shops, cafés and restaurants make informal meeting places. Light showers had made the pavements clean. There was no litter or graffiti. There is a flair and élan to the Venetians as they go about their business.

Venice is not a museum-on-water, but fresh and lively. We saw some of the nicest fruit and vegetables on the street stalls: artichoke hearts floating in water. Perfect aubergines. But we had come to Venice to see the art and architecture. Mostly, we wanted to absorb the Venetian scene.

Venetians are very proud, and so they should be. Venice is magical. You can hardly call the architecture all around you 'buildings', they seem to have risen, white and perfect, out of some classical picture book. From the sea, the pillars with the lion of St Mark and St Theodore (Venice's patron saints) accentuate the famous piazza behind. At the one side there is Sansovino's Library and Mint. The other the pink and white icing of the Ducal Palace with its quatrefoil (four leaved: Matthew, Mark, Luke and John) windows dotting the Gothic lacery.

Everywhere are references to Venice's vanquished foes and to St Mark, the Saints and Mary the Madonna, who saved them from the plague, floods and wars. The four horses of the Basilica, stolen from Constantinople, are said to bring Venice fortune.

Venice of the Italian Renaissance was a time for seeking salvation, for showing riches and power over land and sea. The Domes of the Basilica gently meet the sky, its gems and gold safe inside. Byzantine marbles and gold mosaic icons greet our gaze. St Mark's remains are in the Basilica. He who was told by an angel that here, in Venice, he would find his peace. His symbol, a lion, always holds a book showing the angel's words: *Pax Tibi Marce Evangelist Meus* – Peace to you, Mark my Evangelist.

We were pleasantly surprised that we hadn't had to queue for long – this was a few days before the schools' Easter break. Thursday was our 'Art History' day. Kate and Nina didn't once complain as I swooned over Titian's *Assumption* in the Santa Maria Gloriosa d'Frari. Oh, the beauty of it. Mary herself, spiritually in awe, framed with heavenly gold. Titian used his mosaic training: that a kind of silhouette effect can be wonderfully achieved using light and dark, colour and geometry. Then, next to that *The Pesaro Family,* so that two of the most important works of art of the Italian High Renaissance are just feet from each other.

"And look at the ceiling!" I said. And the same at the Accademia – "Look at the ceiling!" There is some marvellous art literally overlooking you, in Venice and indeed all over the world.

But soon Kate began to make serious murmurings about buying some shoes for her daughter's forthcoming (very swish) party. Also, Nina wanted to look at the meandering canals with their romantic bridges. We all loved to see the *compos*, with washing hung high at top windows with their tiny terraces, dotted with potted plants.

But firstly – a coffee in St Mark's Piazza. Surrounded by classical architecture we order from handsome waiters in black dinner jackets (yes, really). Across the square the waiters at Florians are all in white. The sun came out. We ask a nice Japanese man to take our picture.

We smile at each other. We are in Venice! We made it! Afterwards,

With Nina and Kate

141

we take a long walk along the canals, crossing bridges, taking our time, enjoying the scene. A restaurant looks crowded with working men.

Kate decides that this is a good sign. And indeed, it is. We enter. The sardines are Venetian style, Nina has mussels and survives – Nina can eat and drink anything; Nina eats calamari and grey, unidentified things, with gusto. Kate eats fresh fruit and fish, with plenty of water. Whereas I am a real coward, sticking to monk fish and salad, even worrying if the (perfectly acceptable) red wine will be too acid.

We are getting by with very little Italian, some Spanish, French and a lot of English. We are English women abroad. Well, they are. I am Guernsey so practically European. They laugh at that, though, as I fuss about food and use smiles and hand gestures instead of speaking Italian. Even I know that *Si* and *Grazie* hardly count as joining in wholeheartedly European.

Nina asks for English tea at the Guggenheim and none of us are particularly excited by the museum. It may be that we have already seen quite a few Picassos, Pollocks and Expressionist art. No, the magic of Venice is definitely the art of the Classical and Byzantium, glorious colours and patterns.

We lash out for pre-dinner drinks at the hotel Danieli where the Princess of Wales once stayed. In a room of marbled floors and stairways and sumptuous couches we drink our health. The bill is staggering but we don't care. We all sat back and talked of the past. Nina used to run L'Ancresse Day Nursery where she expertly defused many a child's tantrums. She later ran a guesthouse in St Saviour's. Kate inaugurated a babysitting group, introduced me to *chilli con carne* and wine and breadstick girly evenings, *Nova* and *Spare Rib* (feminist) magazines. Heady stuff in those days, when Guernsey wives hardly ever worked and very few had cars of their own.

Kate became a journalist with the *Guernsey Evening Press* and, to me, was a breath of fresh air. Oh, and the parties we had! Those wonderful uncharted sixties days when women's lives were revolutionised by the contraceptive pill, changing society for ever. But now, we count family and health as most important to us. We have all done our best. We have played the cards we have been dealt. Outside the mists clear Venice, we decide, is truly *Serenissima*.

It is Friday. We leave by Saturday lunchtime. So it's heavy-duty sightseeing. We walk to the Rialto Bridge. It is disappointingly full of tacky stalls. We have never seen so many masks, Murano glassware and theatrical costumes. One of the masks has a long nose. It is the nose of the plague doctor, so he didn't need to get too close to the patient. Poor Venice, plagued by plagues. But she has made up for it.

Lunch again. We walk about, looking for somewhere nice. Ah, this looks good, crowded again with Venetians. In we stride. It is the same restaurant – *Pantalon* – as yesterday! At least we are consistent. Good food, not expensive, good service. A glass or two of wine and we are off again.

On the way back to St Mark's piazza Kate is now determind to buy those shoes. She and Nina get off the waterbus. But I, not really liking shopping, go on to San Zaccaria 'bus stop'. As I meander around the streets I see the Bridge of Sighs. As prisoners left the Ducal Palace of justice, and entered the prison, they sighed. One last look at their beloved Venice.

Kate buys the most elegant pair of dark brown, suede strappy shoes. Nina has bought stamps and postcards and souvenirs. We are ready for our last evening out. Showered and changed we head for Harry's Bar. We nearly do not get our Bellinis (Prosecco and white peach juice) as the waiter shows us to a table, in a very crowded small room. "You have twenty minutes," he instructs us sternly. "No, we don't!" says Kate, heading for the door. She knows her pub staff, this girl and is underwhelmed by their welcome. Nina and I beg her to stay and we gulp our Bellinis. Harry's Bar has its table back in ten minutes.

Then, another very good meal. Although I did send back my fish soup. It arrived looking like an aquarium, full of mussels in shells, octopus and other unmentionable fishy things. I am mindful of my easily irritated holiday tum. Kate and Nina are horrified. How could I? They eat everything put before them.

Next morning I get up very early to finish my film. The piazza is deserted save for other photographers. The air is fresh and still. It is going to be a sunny day. The sea laps the gondolas. I think again of how mysterious Venice is. It is so much more than a beautiful face, Queen of the Adriatic.

We all want to go back to do the Accademia properly, see the Ducal Palace, San Giorgio Maggiore, the Salute, Ca' d'Oro… many other things. We have, in no way, 'done' Venice.

For our last morning we went to the San Zaccaria church which holds a sublime Bellini painting *Madonna and Child with Saints*. It is perfect in proportion, wonderful in colour and in an historically fascinating building, not to be missed.

And so we begin our journey home. This time we have conquered the waterbus, the coach terminus and Treviso airport. A seasoned traveller, Kate finds a café in the sunshine near the airport. We down cases and sit for an hour in a warm corner instead of sitting bored stiff in the stuffy departure lounge.

We recall our conversations and reminiscences. I thank them for listening to me when I told of some recent painful difficulties. "That's what friends are for," says Nina, remembering one of the books she used to read to her charges at the L'Ancresse Day Nursery. "And don't," said Kate, "forget to look at the ceiling!" Take three girls.

38 Guernsey Literature and Potato Peel Pie

September 2009

Next year, 2010, it will be 70 years since our dear island was occupied by the enemy forces of Germany during World War Two. Much has been written about the Occupation: by people who survived it and evacuees who were separated from their homes for five years. Writers have imagined what an extraordinary time it was for all the Channel Islands.

One such writer is the American, Mary Ann Shaffer. Another is Gerald Basil Edwards, born in Guernsey. Shaffer wrote the now very famous *The Guernsey Literary and Potato Peel Pie Society*, Edwards wrote the equally successful *The Book of Ebenezer Le Page*. Both books are impeccably researched and both have a strong romantic story to tell.

However, their styles are very different. Where Edwards' story is told in the first person, over seven decades, Shaffer uses the fictional device of epistolary (letters tell the tale). Shaffer captures the hard times people endured as the German regime inevitably slowly bore down on them, eventually bringing all islanders, captive and captors, to near starvation. She has a highly engaging style and her characters are skilfully drawn; the plot of the book is compelling and the ending satisfying. Shaffer does not hold back on her descriptions of the unbelievable atrocities such as those carried out on slave workers and in concentration camps. It is important that our island history is recorded in this way.

My one, and it is only one, criticism is that the timbre of the voices of the island people do not ring true to me. This is a shame because in fact only Guernsey people lived on the island during the Occupation. Foreign born – including English, which is why my mother had to leave with her four month old baby – were forced to leave or be forcibly deported.

G.B. Edwards, who was born in Guernsey and lived here until he was in his late teens, does capture the unique, salty humour and wry, sage speech that fellow islanders recognise. Many of our relations stayed during the Occupation: my late father-in-law, Claude Ozanne, his brother-in-law,

James Carré; grandparents, great aunts and uncles.

We heard their stories first-hand. They were of hunger, fear and great loneliness. But their stoical, true Guernsey donkey spirit got them through. Here are some excerpts from heavily censored letters sent to and from loved ones who would not see each other for so many, long years:

"Dearest, Always thinking of you. Longing for reunion."
"Sweet memories. Hopes for future, my comfort."
"Yearning just for you."
"Dawn is breaking. Daylight spreading. We are waiting."

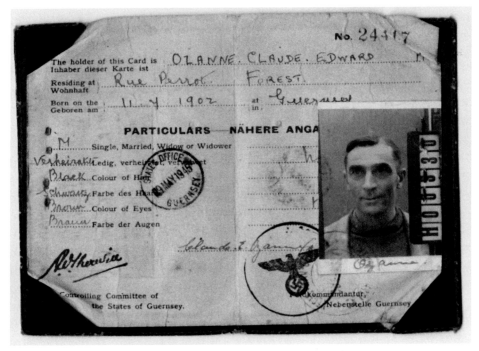

Claude Ozanne's Identity Card

Claude Ozanne told us that boredom and loneliness were the worst things, then hunger, which became permanent as the years went on. James Carré invented a blancmange made from *vraic* (seaweed). He had a chemist's training and he sold his 'Carravita' powder over the counter. He also made tooth powder out of cuttle fish, powdered and flavoured with carbolic or peppermint; also egg and baking powder to his own formulas.

The illicit keeping of pigs during the severe rationing of the Second World War is related in both Shaffer's and Edwards' stories. Ebenezer's exploits came first, when the book was published in 1981. All keepers of pigs were subjected to a tally. The islanders thought of several ways in which to trick their adversaries, but: 'Judge my horror when Mr Tom Ozanne, who had to do with the Controlling Committee turned up one fine day with a German Officer and of course, a book and a pencil.' There follows a hilarious account of how Ebenezer and his neighbours outwitted their enemy.

At the very core of *The Guernsey Literary and Potato Peel Pie Society* (the reason for its existence) is the story of a roast-pig dinner. 'Mrs Maugery' has hidden a pig, then killed it for dinner. Since a pig is a fairly large animal (it was actually usually salted and stored on a rack from the kitchen ceiling; cuts would be taken when needed). 'Mrs Maugery' invites some friends round to eat it. Unfortunately, on the way home, amidst the merriment, they miss the imposed curfew and are challenged by German patrol officers. Breaking curfew is a very serious offence. The quick-witted (key character) 'Elizabeth' immediately protests that they had all been to a meeting of the Guernsey Literary Society (as yet unformed). But the Society does indeed form, with the potato peel pie (hungry people are inventive) later being added as sustenance whilst the members discussed their books. Shaffer includes an account of the German officer's tallies and the methods that were employed by pig keepers to bamboozle the Germans. These accounts are very similar to those first included in *Ebenezer*. The telling of assisting a young slave worker (again, punishable by being shot or sent to a concentration camp) also appears in both books.

Let me make it clear: I much enjoyed reading *The Guernsey Literary and Potato Peel Pie Society*; it is a warm, intelligent and informative read. But where *Ebenezer Le Page* is immersed in Guernsey culture, with Norman French surnames, the contemplative mind and the 'Guernsey wink' that John Fowles speaks of, I much missed these in Shaffer's book. Her hero 'Dawsey Adams' (a crucial character) appears, to me, as an Englishman with an English name. Although she certainly doesn't paint islanders as village buffoons and her character 'Isola Pribby' is genuinely comic (although I didn't care for her name, either) something important is missing. To explain: think of how different *Under Milk Wood* by Dylan Thomas would read if it were not in the Welsh lilting voice. Anything by

Edna O'Brien has an air of Irish beguilement.

We came back to the island in 1946. It was bloodied but unbowed. Like Shaffer's 'Juliet' I am totally in awe of how Guernsey and all the Channel Islands' people not only survived but reunited. Together they buckled to and strove forward.

Since 1940, many stories have been told about the Occupation of our dear islands. They are worth repeating, especially to those who were unaware of the ravages that war brings to a small, peaceful community. We can never forget.

39 Tide and Time

February 2008

The other day I thought I had found my first violet of spring. Excited, I rummaged around in the leaves and grass, only to see that it was a Quality Street purple wrapper: the one with soft toffee and a nut in it. It was scrunched up and empty so I didn't even get to eat the chocolate. Still, spring is most definitely on its way, thank goodness. There are daffodils and primroses burgeoning everywhere – a gladdening sight in our wintry fields and hedges.

February 2nd is Candlemas Day, a time when a mass is said to bless the Church candles for the coming year. February is the beginning of Lent and it is a cleansing, fasting time. It is the mid-point of winter, halfway between the shortest day and the spring equinox. So at least we are half-way to the sunnier days and Easter is very early this year.

Last Sunday it might have been summer, the sun was so warm. An orange sun setting by Lihou Island made the incoming tide streak pink, shimmering into pale lavender. We onlookers, perched near the Prosperity Memorial, watched three people on the island suddenly realising that the tide was coming in fast, so began scurrying across the causeway. We didn't take our eyes off them, watching as they slipped and slid over the *vraic*-strewn, pebbly path until they had reached the cobbled slipway. They made it, just in time. We all smiled.

The onrushing waves made me think of the Alderney Race, where the sea rushes in fast as a speedboat. It has a rise and fall of 40 feet. And that made me think of Hugh Fearnley-Whittingstall and his recent programme on the Channel Islands. I couldn't help feeling a bit sorry for the man and his mates as they somewhat tentatively ate raw limpets. Did they not think of washing them first, then throwing them on a fire for a few minutes?

People did that in the past. Guernsey people went shrimping, as well, waiting for the turn of a low tide then scooping up plump shrimps in nets. The bounty would be washed with water brought specially for the venture. Then a small fire, sheltered by stones, would be made and the shrimps devoured with fresh bread there and then.

Edwin ('Winno') Bréhaut

Tide and Time

Our huge tides bring a whole selection of seafood, there for our taking. Moonlit nights reveal sandeels, popping out of the sand. On a good night the sand fairly gleams with the wet and shimmery fish. All we have to do is go down to the beach with forks and a bucket and collect them. You must get hold of Marguerite Paul's splendid books about our islands fish, including all shellfish, if you want to know how to cook eels, congers or just about anything else from around our shores.

My mother was a great cockler. At very low tide she used to go down to L'Islet with some of her grandchildren, buckets and rakes. It was nothing to collect two or three dozen cockles. The sea was so far out, you could see the beaches of Rousse, Les Amarreurs and Chouet. Once home my mother would soak the cockles in cold water to extract the sand then cook them with a little water for ten to fifteen minutes. The cockles would open their shells then she would drain them in a colander to get rid of any remaining sand. They are best eaten plainly, with vinegar and bread and butter. Delicious. Mary says they taste a bit like oysters but I have never eaten oysters so I will take her word for it.

However, much to my father's disgust, I never did like conger eel even if it had been poached in milk. The flesh was alright but I have always disliked the smell of the beast. My father said that the biggest conger eels were often in the same vicinity as lobsters. Both creatures like deep, dark places. I can't say that makes me want to cook congers any the more but I am very partial to a lobster. We were told not to eat lobsters hot. For our best digestion, lobsters should be eaten cold. So I never told my father that I liked Lobster Thermidor, cooked with a creamy cheese sauce, best of all.

A fair deal has been written about ormers so I won't add a lot more about them except that they are probably the most tasty of all our molluscs. My father used to catch huge quantities of the things from his secret place near the end of Chouet. You have to go a good way out in the cold sea with your ormering hook if you want a good feed. Once home, the business of scrubbing the black frilly edges began the pre-cooking process. Then on a stone slab with a huge wooden mallet (kept by Great Aunt Elise especially for this job) the ormers were beaten to an edible thinness.

Then came the mouth-watering smell as the ormers, dipped in flour, were fried in butter. Absolute gourmet heaven. Some people prefer ormers pickled in vinegar, others like ormer casserole, but as I write this and think of those fried ones I am licking my lips. It is no good, Tony will have to get an ormering hook and we will see if we can find the place my father went to....

As we left Lihou Island behind, the tide, which had been very low, was rising now to silver smooth at one side, rolling incoming waves coming in from the other. Dusk approached, turning Portelet's pine-trees into a silhouette, the headland forming a dark cove against the now lowering sky of crimson. Where Portelet's shadow fell into the sea, it shone like a glassy green mirror.

All of this can be found on one sunny day in Guernsey. Such stunning beauty and wonderful food is within everyone's reach, old or young. Just think, soon the violets will be with us. This time they will be real.

40   Mary Bréhaut

July 2008

Mary Bréhaut, died on May 1st. I know that a lot of people knew my mother, so I hope you that you will understand if I dedicate this article to her. When my book *Love Apple Island* was published, my mother was delighted, especially with a photograph of us both together, taken shopping in Town in the Forties. I must have been around five and my mother only 27 although already a mother of three young children.

Mary began her life in Bury, Lancashire, of Irish parentage. She wasn't a strong child but after convalescent caring she joined her two sisters at Hollymount, a Roman Catholic Convent. Hollymount was Mary's home until she was sixteen. The dedicated nuns taught literature, music, lace-making and needlework, which Mary excelled in.

After the First World War ended, Mary told me how she had witnessed weary soldiers returning to England. Destitute men were given food, clothes and money from the nuns. Once, Mary saw a man, dressed in rags, limping along the long path through the fields to the Convent. Exhausted, he leaned on the front door and was taken in immediately.

The Convent was virtually self-sufficient, with its own farm, vegetable garden, laundry and a chapel. The excellent little school where the girls were taught had a library stocked with the classics of literature, poetry and plays. Some of the nuns were of European aristocracy and all of the teachers were highly vocational.

Mum used to laugh when she related that all the 'good' girls were allowed an annual holiday to Blackpool. The second list were given a whole day's outing somewhere and the 'naughty' ones had just a trip to the local cinema. Mum never made it past the cinema trip. But she retained a life-long love of good drama and was never bitter about anything.

In fact, it was a strength all her life – Mary didn't ever dwell on what might have been, or, indeed, at times, what ought to have been. Mary always looked forward with a great spirit of heart and acceptance of the – sometimes – rather hard lot life had dealt her.

Mary used to read us bedtime stories. She could recite poems by heart, learnt from Hollymount. One I have always loved was told to us in her light, warm voice and began:

'The fairies have never a penny to spend
they haven't a thing put by.
But theirs is the dower
Of bird and flower
And theirs are the earth and the sky...'

Another verse Mary loved to tell always amused us:

'I dreamt I did die
And to Heaven did go
Where had I come from?
They wanted to know
When I said Hollymount
My they did stare.
'Come in! cried Saint Peter
You're the first one from there!'

My mother would take us to the the Little Theatre to see the Dotrice family and the Dennison Players. We watched many a play on our black and white television with her. I enjoyed the drama series best: *Sense and Sensibility, Vanity Fair* and saw many superb plays. Alan Badel was the heart-throb in those days – a kind of Fifties Colin Firth. Mr Badel seemed to be in practically everything and I thought he was most handsome.

As time went by and we had grown up, Mary took great pleasure in attending all her social and church groups. She regularly went to Jubilee House, to the Russells, at Les Côtils, and the Guernsey Blind Association. We joked that she had a busier social life than we did. In fact, this was not altogether untrue. After our father died, Mary's fellowship meetings and attending the Methodist church of St Paul's became more important to her.

She studied The Minor Prophets when she was over 80 years-old. Mary gained an astonishing 92.5% for her work on such prophets as Obadiah and Habakkuk. Often, she could quote the Bible to you word for word. As her children, grandchildren, great and great-great grandchildren we were able to take much comfort from our mother's words. She always

Mary, 19, and Edwin Bréhaut, 26

Left: Edwin and Mary, née Long, St Joseph's Church, 1939
Right: Diamond Wedding, 1999

had wise counsel to give and unending time for anyone and everyone.

For the last year of her life, Mary lived at Gardenia Lodge, a residential home for the elderly. She soon made some very close friends and was a lively and enthusiastic contributor to all that was going on around her. Even as she became frail of body, her compassion for everyone never waned. She taught me, especially, that it is to the weak and the defenceless to whom we must show mercy and whom we must help.

Earthly riches never meant anything to Mary. She owned no precious jewellery nor expensive finery, but saw beauty in a meadow full of wild flowers. Our favourite drive was all around Les Mielles, at the most northern tip of Guernsey. Here, I would stop the car and we would wind down the windows and listen to a skylark and watch the grasses stir in the breeze. A little further on and we would park to look over the tiny island of Houmet Paradis, the tiny microcosm of Guernsey that Victor Hugo so powerfully wrote of. Then, Bordeaux with its unbeatable views of Herm, Sark, Alderney and even Jersey: all the Channel Islands, in fact.

There is, said Mary, something spiritual about this place. 'I felt it the minute I came to Guernsey. I knew that I would live here all my life.'

To 'What do you say? What evidence Is there in your life that you have a genuine relationship with God?' Mary answered in her writing:

'Through prayers, meditation, study and learning (and listening) to and of the scriptures, trying hard to obey God's will – I now feel as if I am a truly genuine child of God.'

Yes, you were, our mother Mary. You were a truly genuine child of God and we thank Him for your life and for your love for us that is still with us and always will be.

41 A Matter of Manners

April 2009

One of the most insidious changes in Guernsey society since we were young is the lack of respect shown to people and property. This lack of manners appears in many ways: a pedestrian strolling in front of oncoming traffic looking neither left nor right, forcing a driver to take evasive action. Or a car parked so closely to another the owner can hardly get into his vehicle. We were taught to 'Look right, look left, look right again then proceed if it is safe.' And isn't it common courtesy to leave room for someone – possibly with children and shopping – to comfortably enter their own car? But of course, these small respects involve using a bit of consideration for others. Heaven forbid.

A cinema trip can be made a misery if the person next to you chats to her friend, whilst chomping through crackling packets of crisps, popcorn and chocolates – throughout the entire film. Again, people talk loudly into mobile phones in public places like shops, completely ignoring those next to them. Sometimes they even do this whilst being served. Put together, acts like these are divisive and excluding; they lessen our sense of community and damage the concept of individuals involving themselves in a common identity.

The structure of society has radically changed. We always addressed our teachers as Mrs, Miss and Mr. In my first job all the bosses were called Mr. We wouldn't have dreamt of calling people by their Christian names unless invited to do so. Even the word 'Christian' has been ambushed by the PC brigade, so that now we are asked for our 'first name' when form filling.

A visit from my grandmother was a serious business. A chair would be found for her where she would sit, centre of attention, examining us about school, the clothes we wore, all with a stern, beady eye for anything she didn't like. Dressed all in black, as befitting a widow, my grandmother sipped a cup of tea, expecting, and receiving, a respectful audience. Any behaviour she didn't approve of was reported to my father when he came home. She lived until 100 years old and I remember her telling my mother (who was 70 at the time and had been married for 50 years) precisely how my father (her son) liked his vegetables cooked. Her favourite phrase, when she wasn't speaking Guernsey patois, was 'Don't leave me keep you,' meaning 'get on with your work'. Nobody argued. After all she was our elder and, unquestionably, head of our family.

Grandmother would be disgusted to hear some of the language used freely these days. As for answering adults back this was absolutely unheard of. Rudeness was punished. Control was kept by discipline because discipline was not, in those days, seen as denying a child the right to behave exactly as it wished.

Yet, in a well-ordered, respectful community everyone has rights, including the elderly. We children knew what to expect should we wilfully break the rules: a denial of privileges, the cane, detention, shunned by those who disapproved of us. Criminal wrongdoing by an adolescent could result in six strokes of the birch. No culprit ever returned for a second time, I do assure you.

Very gradually, some anti-social behaviour has permeated our Guernsey way of life. Visit Town on a Saturday afternoon and you will hear obscenities once only heard late at night and even then in the seedier haunts. This, from groups of teenage boys and girls openly talking about the drugs they are taking and each other's sex lives. It is just plain sad to see and hear young Guernsey girls and boys spoiling themselves with such ugly behaviour.

Since for some, obedience, pride and conformity is jeered at, it must be difficult for their teachers to enforce restrictions. Some parents have woeful standards of discipline in the home, anyway, so how then can the police, also, be expected to deal with a breakdown of authority? Police must be sick of dealing with kids with no fear of reprisal or challenged for their actions and with no acceptance of consequences or responsibility.

In today's climate it can also be hard going to teach Christian, moral, values to young people. I am talking here of kindness, decency, tolerance and allowing other people their dignity and right to be safe. Who would have thought that these simple, basic values would have become so eroded, so scorned, so swiftly? But once adults devalue what they perceive as old-fashioned, children will readily follow.

If the example of adults, by condoning anti-social acts, or at least doing little to stop them, is what younger people see day in and day out, why should they care? Indeed, how can they change? Take 'old-fashioned'

Great grandmother Henriette (Harriet) Heaume, 1914

values away, like honour and loyalty – what will be put in their place? Nothing, that's what.

When the media lowered the barriers of accepted decency, society – yes, even Guernsey society – has, inevitably, paid the price. It is not fashionable to say so and I may be accused of being a killjoy, but do we really have to view crude nudity and hear blasphemous (another word deemed outdated) language inflicted upon us every day and everywhere?

We are never going back, I realise that, to an accepted reverence of authority. There will always be those who despise people in power, however hard they have worked to get there and, or, been democratically elected. Successful people will always be accused of elitism. Jealousy is one of mankind's most dangerous and corrosive of sins.

Drugs are here to stay and the culture of 'anything goes' that accompanies them. Maybe, though, future generations, sick of the diminishing quality of their lives and undoubtedly needing help, will think again and gather together the teachings on what used to matter and why.

I believe that this will, eventually, happen. In the meantime, let's have faith, hope and charity. For the human condition will always need these and they never go out of fashion.

Until the next time, *à la perchoin*.